Regionals E-Campus
4200 N University Blvd
Middletown OH 45042

W9-DCC-753

MIAMI REGIONALS E-CAMPUS

GLENN    GEORGE

BRIAN    JIM    JOE    DAVE

VAL    JOE    CHRIS    NELSON

GORDON    BARRY

WALT DISNEP Imagineering

IMAGINEERS

WHERE DREAMS COME TRUE

JESS    JOHN

OWEN    AILEEN    JIM    OMAR

BOB    GOOFY    TIM    DANIEL

ALFREDO    TOM    KATHY    OSCAR

CHRIS    DIEGO    DAVE    CORY

FINTAN    LANNY    JOHN    BRUCE

COMMUNICATE WITH VISUAL LITERACY • DISNEY PARK EXPERIENCE • 6 AVOID OVERLOAD—CREATE TURN-ONS • 2 WEAR YOUR GUESTS' SHOES • PASSION • 3 ORGANIZE THE FLOW OF PEOPLE AND IDEAS • MENTOR • THINK DIFFERENTLY • 9 FOR EVERY OUNCE OF TREATMENT, PROVIDE A TON OF TREAT • BECOME THE BEST • 10 KEEP IT UP (MAINTAIN IT)! • TURN-ONS • EDUCATION—NEVER STOP LEARNING • 7 TELL ONE STORY AT A TIME • BE CURIOUS • 8 AVOID CONTRADICTIONS—MAINTAIN IDENTITY • MENTOR • 4 CREATE A WIENIE (VISUAL MAGNET) • COLLABORATION • 5 COMMUNICATE WITH VISUAL LITERACY • 10 KEEP IT UP (MAINTAIN IT)! • 1 KNOW YOUR AUDIENCE • STORY • 2 WEAR YOUR GUESTS' SHOES • PASSION • AVOID CONTRADICTIONS—MAINTAIN IDENTITY • TAKE A CHANCE / THINK DIFFERENTLY • 9 FOR EVERY OUNCE OF TREATMENT • LITERACY • DISNEY PARK EXPERIENCE • 6 AVOID OVERLOAD—CREATE TURN-ONS • EDUCATION—NEVER STOP LEARNING • SHOES • PASSION • 3 ORGANIZE THE FLOW OF PEOPLE AND IDEAS • MENTOR • 4 CREATE A WIENIE (VISUAL MAGNET) • Y OUNCE OF TREATMENT, PROVIDE A TON OF TREAT • BECOME THE BEST • 10 KEEP IT UP (MAINTAIN IT)! • NEVER STOP LEARNING • 7 TELL ONE STORY AT A TIME • BE CURIOUS • 8 AVOID CONTRADICTIONS—MAINTAIN IDENTITY • WIENIE (VISUAL MAGNET) • COLLABORATION • 5 COMMUNICATE WITH VISUAL LITERACY • DISNEY PARK EXPERIENCE • MAINTAIN IT)! • 1 KNOW YOUR AUDIENCE • STORY • 2 WEAR YOUR GUESTS' SHOES • PASSION • 3 ORGANIZE • CTIONS—MAINTAIN IDENTITY • TAKE A CHANCE / THINK DIFFERENTLY • 9 FOR EVERY OUNCE OF TREATMENT, • SNEY PARK EXPERIENCE • 6 AVOID OVERLOAD—CREATE TURN-ONS • EDUCATION—NEVER STOP LEARNING • ON • 3 ORGANIZE THE FLOW OF PEOPLE AND IDEAS • MENTOR • 4 CREATE A WIENIE (VISUAL MAGNET) • C TREATMENT, PROVIDE A TON OF TREAT • BECOME THE BEST • 10 KEEP IT UP (MAINTAIN IT)! • 1 KNOW YOUR NING • 7 TELL ONE STORY AT A TIME • BE CURIOUS • 8 AVOID CONTRADICTIONS—MAINTAIN IDENTITY • TAK NET) • COLLABORATION • 5 COMMUNICATE WITH VISUAL LITERACY • DISNEY PARK EXPERIENCE • 6 AVOID O YOUR AUDIENCE • STORY • 2 WEAR YOUR GUESTS' SHOES • PASSION • 3 ORGANIZE THE FLOW OF PEOPLE TY • TAKE A CHANCE / THINK DIFFERENTLY • 9 FOR EVERY OUNCE OF TREATMENT, PROVIDE A TON OF TREAT AVOID OVERLOAD—CREATE TURN-ONS • EDUCATION—NEVER STOP LEARNING • 7 TELL ONE STORY AT A TIME OF PEOPLE AND IDEAS • MENTOR • 4 CREATE A WIENIE (VISUAL MAGNET) • COLLABORATION • 5 COMMU OF TREAT • BECOME THE BEST • 10 KEEP IT UP (MAINTAIN IT)! • 1 KNOW YOUR AUDIENCE • STORY • 2 WEAR A TIME • BE CURIOUS • 8 AVOID CONTRADICTIONS—MAINTAIN IDENTITY • TAKE A CHANCE / THINK DIFFE COMMUNICATE WITH VISUAL LITERACY • DISNEY PARK EXPERIENCE • 6 AVOID OVERLOAD—CREATE TURN-ON Y • 2 WEAR YOUR GUESTS' SHOES • PASSION • 3 ORGANIZE THE FLOW OF PEOPLE AND IDEAS • MENTOR • INK DIFFERENTLY • 9 FOR EVERY OUNCE OF TREATMENT, PROVIDE A TON OF TREAT • BECOME THE BEST • 10 TURN-ONS • EDUCATION—NEVER STOP LEARNING • 7 TELL ONE STORY AT A TIME • BE CURIOUS • 8 AVOID NTOR • 4 CREATE A WIENIE (VISUAL MAGNET) • COLLABORATION • 5 COMMUNICATE WITH VISUAL LITERAC T • 10 KEEP IT UP (MAINTAIN IT)! • 1 KNOW YOUR AUDIENCE • STORY • 2 WEAR YOUR GUESTS' SHOES • PAS ID CONTRADICTIONS—MAINTAIN IDENTITY • TAKE A CHANCE / THINK DIFFERENTLY • 9 FOR EVERY OUNCE TERACY • DISNEY PARK EXPERIENCE • 6 AVOID OVERLOAD—CREATE TURN-ONS • EDUCATION—NEVER STOP ES • PASSION • 3 ORGANIZE THE FLOW OF PEOPLE AND IDEAS • MENTOR • 4 CREATE A WIENIE (VISUAL Y OUNCE OF TREATMENT, PROVIDE A TON OF TREAT • BECOME THE BEST • 10 KEEP IT UP (MAINTAIN

# One Little Spark!

## Mickey's Ten Commandments
### and The Road to Imagineering

...RK EXPE
...ION • 3 ORGAN
...UNCE OF TREATMENT, P
...—NEVER STOP LEARNING • 7 TE
...A WIENIE (VISUAL MAGNET) • COLLABO
...EEP IT UP (MAINTAIN IT)! • 1 KNOW YOUR AUDI
...AVOID CONTRADICTIONS—MAINTAIN IDENTITY • TAKE A C
...LITERACY · DISM... ...ARK EXPERIENCE · 8 AVOID OVERLOAD

COMMUNICATE WITH VISUAL LITERACY • DISNEY PARK EXPERIENCE • 6 AVOID OVERLOAD—CREATE TURN-ON
Y • 2 WEAR YOUR GUESTS' SHOES • PASSION • 3 ORGANIZE THE FLOW OF PEOPLE AND IDEAS • MENTOR •
NK DIFFERENTLY • 9 FOR EVERY OUNCE OF TREATMENT, PROVIDE A TON OF TREAT • BECOME THE BEST • 10 K
RN-ONS • EDUCATION—NEVER STOP LEARNING • 7 TELL ONE STORY AT A TIME • BE CURIOUS • 8 AVOID CO
NTOR • 4 CREATE A WIENIE (VISUAL MAGNET) • COLLABORATION • 5 COMMUNICATE WITH VISUAL LITERACY
• 10 KEEP IT UP (MAINTAIN IT)! • 1 KNOW YOUR AUDIENCE • STORY • 2 WEAR YOUR GUESTS' SHOES • PAS
D CONTRADICTIONS—MAINTAIN IDENTITY • TAKE A CHANCE / THINK DIFFERENTLY • 9 FOR EVERY OUNCE OF
ERACY • DISNEY PARK EXPERIENCE • 6 AVOID OVERLOAD—CREATE TURN-ONS • EDUCATION—NEVER STOP LE
ES • PASSION • 3 ORGANIZE THE FLOW OF PEOPLE AND IDEAS • MENTOR • 4 CREATE A WIENIE (VISUAL MA
OUNCE OF TREATMENT, PROVIDE A TON OF TREAT • BECOME THE BEST • 10 KEEP IT UP (MAINTAIN IT)! • 1
EVER STOP LEARNING • 7 TELL ONE STORY AT A TIME • BE CURIOUS • 8 AVOID CONTRADICTIONS—MAINTAI
NIE (VISUAL MAGNET) • COLLABORATION • 5 COMMUNICATE WITH VISUAL LITERACY • DISNEY PARK EXPERI
AINTAIN IT)! • 1 KNOW YOUR AUDIENCE • STORY • 2 WEAR YOUR GUESTS' SHOES • PASSION • 3 ORGANIZ
CTIONS—MAINTAIN IDENTITY • TAKE A CHANCE / THINK DIFFERENTLY • 9 FOR EVERY OUNCE OF TREATMENT,
NEY PARK EXPERIENCE • 6 AVOID OVERLOAD—CREATE TURN-ONS • EDUCATION—NEVER STOP LEARNING • 7
ON • 3 ORGANIZE THE FLOW OF PEOPLE AND IDEAS • MENTOR • 4 CREATE A WIENIE (VISUAL MAGNET) • CO
TREATMENT, PROVIDE A TON OF TREAT • BECOME THE BEST • 10 KEEP IT UP (MAINTAIN IT)! • 1 KNOW YOUR A
ING • 7 TELL ONE STORY AT A TIME • BE CURIOUS • 8 AVOID CONTRADICTIONS—MAINTAIN IDENTITY • TAK
ET) • COLLABORATION • 5 COMMUNICATE WITH VISUAL LITERACY • DISNEY PARK EXPERIENCE • 6 AVOID OV
YOUR AUDIENCE • STORY • 2 WEAR YOUR GUESTS' SHOES • PASSION • 3 ORGANIZE THE FLOW OF PEOPLE
Y • TAKE A CHANCE / THINK DIFFERENTLY • 9 FOR EVERY OUNCE OF TREATMENT, PROVIDE A TON OF TREAT •
AVOID OVERLOAD—CREATE TURN-ONS • EDUCATION—NEVER STOP LEARNING • 7 TELL ONE STORY AT A TIME
OF PEOPLE AND IDEAS • MENTOR • 4 CREATE A WIENIE (VISUAL MAGNET) • COLLABORATION • 5 COMMUN
F TREAT • BECOME THE BEST • 10 KEEP IT UP (MAINTAIN IT)! • 1 KNOW YOUR AUDIENCE • STORY • 2 WEAR
A TIME • BE CURIOUS • 8 AVOID CONTRADICTIONS—MAINTAIN IDENTITY • TAKE A CHANCE / THINK DIFFERE
COMMUNICATE WITH VISUAL LITERACY • DISNEY PARK EXPERIENCE • 6 AVOID OVERLOAD—CREATE TURN-ONS
Y • 2 WEAR YOUR GUESTS' SHOES • PASSION • 3 ORGANIZE THE FLOW OF PEOPLE AND IDEAS • MENTOR •
NK DIFFERENTLY • 9 FOR EVERY OUNCE OF TREATMENT, PROVIDE A TON OF TREAT • BECOME THE BEST • 10 K
RN-ONS • EDUCATION—NEVER STOP LEARNING • 7 TELL ONE STORY AT A TIME • BE CURIOUS • 8 AVOID CO
NTOR • 4 CREATE A WIENIE (VISUAL MAGNET) • COLLABORATION • 5 COMMUNICATE WITH VISUAL LITERACY
• 10 KEEP IT UP (MAINTAIN IT)! • 1 KNOW YOUR AUDIENCE • STORY • 2 WEAR YOUR GUESTS' SHOES • PASS
D CONTRADICTIONS—MAINTAIN IDENTITY • TAKE A CHANCE / THINK DIFFERENTLY • 9 FOR EVERY OUNCE OF
ERACY • DISNEY PARK EXPERIENCE • 6 AVOID OVERLOAD—CREATE TURN-ONS • EDUCATION—NEVER STOP LE
ES • PASSION • 3 ORGANIZE THE FLOW OF PEOPLE AND IDEAS • MENTOR • 4 CREATE A WIENIE (VISUAL MA
OUNCE OF TREATMENT, PROVIDE A TON OF TREAT • BECOME THE BEST • 10 KEEP IT UP (MAINTAIN IT)!

# One Little Spark!

## Mickey's Ten Commandments and The Road to Imagineering

By **Marty Sklar**
Disney Legend and Imagineering Ambassador

Edited by **Leslie Sklar**

Introductions by **Richard M. Sherman** and **Glen Keane**

**Disney EDITIONS**

Los Angeles • New York

Copyright © 2015 Marty Sklar Creative, Inc.

All rights reserved. Published by Disney Editions, an imprint of Disney Book Group. No part of this book may be reproduced or transmitted in any form or by any means, electronic or mechanical, including photocopying, recording, or by any information storage and retrieval system, without written permission from the publisher.

For information address Disney Editions, 1101 Flower Street, Glendale, California 91201

One Little Spark
Words and Music by Richard Sherman and Robert Sherman
© 1981 Wonderland Music Company, Inc. (BMI)
All Rights Reserved. Used With Permission.

Meet The World
Words and Music by Richard Sherman and Robert Sherman
© 1982 Wonderland Music Company, Inc. (BMI)
All Rights Reserved. Used With Permission.

There's A Great Big Beautiful Tomorrow
Words and Music by Richard Sherman and Robert Sherman
© 1963 Wonderland Music Company, Inc. (BMI)
Copyright Renewed. All Rights Reserved. Used With Permission.

It's A Small World
Words and Music by Richard Sherman and Robert Sherman
© 1963 Wonderland Music Company, Inc. (BMI)
Copyright Renewed. All Rights Reserved. Used With Permission.

Academy Award® and Oscar® are registered trademarks of the
Academy of Motion Picture Arts and Sciences

Library of Congress Cataloging-in-Publication Data

Sklar, Marty.
 One little spark : Mickey's ten commandments and the road to imagineering / by
Marty Sklar ; edited by Leslie Sklar ; introductions by Richard M. Sherman and Glen Keane. —
First edition.
    pages cm
 Includes index.
 ISBN 978-1-4847-3763-7
 1. Walt Disney Company. 2. Creative ability. I. Sklar, Leslie. II. Imagineers (Group) III. Title.
 PN1999.W27S55 2015
 791.06'8—dc23
                    2014049757

FAC-020093-15198
Printed in the United States / First Edition, September 2015
10 9 8 7 6 5 4 3 2 1
ISBN 978-1-4847-3763-7

THIS LABEL APPLIES TO TEXT STOCK

For John Hench, Herb Ryman,
Richard Irvine, and all my mentors at
Walt Disney Imagineering.
The Disney Legends taught me the "magic
formula"—I have been spreading Pixie Dust
in their memory ever since.

And for
Leslie Sklar,
Rachel and Jacob Dahan,
and
Howard Sklar,
Katriina Koski-Sklar,
and Gabriel and Hannah Sklar.

And my one and only love,
Leah Gerber Sklar,
who made my career
and life
a dream come true.

COMMUNICATE WITH VISUAL LITERACY • DISNEY PARK EXPERIENCE • 6 AVOID OVERLOAD–CREATE TURN-ONS
• 2 WEAR YOUR GUESTS' SHOES • PASSION • 3 ORGANIZE THE FLOW OF PEOPLE AND IDEAS • MENTOR •
NK DIFFERENTLY • 9 FOR EVERY OUNCE OF TREATMENT, PROVIDE A TON OF TREAT • BECOME THE BEST • 10 K
RN-ONS • EDUCATION–NEVER STOP LEARNING • 7 TELL ONE STORY AT A TIME • BE CURIOUS • 8 AVOID CO
NTOR • 4 CREATE A WIENIE (VISUAL MAGNET) • COLLABORATION • 5 COMMUNICATE WITH VISUAL LITERACY
• 10 KEEP IT UP (MAINTAIN IT)! • 1 KNOW YOUR AUDIENCE • STORY • 2 WEAR YOUR GUESTS' SHOES • PASS
D CONTRADICTIONS–MAINTAIN IDENTITY • TAKE A CHANCE / THINK DIFFERENTLY • 9 FOR EVERY OUNCE OF
ERACY • DISNEY PARK EXPERIENCE • 6 AVOID OVERLOAD–CREATE TURN-ONS • EDUCATION–NEVER STOP LE
S • PASSION • 3 ORGANIZE THE FLOW OF PEOPLE AND IDEAS • MENTOR • 4 CREATE A WIENIE (VISUAL MA
OUNCE OF TREATMENT, PROVIDE A TON OF TREAT • BECOME THE BEST • 10 KEEP IT UP (MAINTAIN IT)! • 1
EVER STOP LEARNING • 7 TELL ONE STORY AT A TIME • BE CURIOUS • 8 AVOID CONTRADICTIONS–MAINTAI
NIE (VISUAL MAGNET) • COLLABORATION • 5 COMMUNICATE WITH VISUAL LITERACY • DISNEY PARK EXPERI
AINTAIN IT)! • 1 KNOW YOUR AUDIENCE • STORY • 2 WEAR YOUR GUESTS' SHOES • PASSION • 3 ORGANIZ
TIONS–MAINTAIN IDENTITY • TAKE A CHANCE / THINK DIFFERENTLY • 9 FOR EVERY OUNCE OF TREATMENT,
NEY PARK EXPERIENCE • 6 AVOID OVERLOAD–CREATE TURN-ONS • EDUCATION–NEVER STOP LEARNING • 7
ON • 3 ORGANIZE THE FLOW OF PEOPLE AND IDEAS • MENTOR • 4 CREATE A WIENIE (VISUAL MAGNET) • CC
REATMENT, PROVIDE A TON OF TREAT • BECOME THE BEST • 10 KEEP IT UP (MAINTAIN IT)! • 1 KNOW YOUR A
ING • 7 TELL ONE STORY AT A TIME • BE CURIOUS • 8 AVOID CONTRADICTIONS–MAINTAIN IDENTITY • TAKE
ET) • COLLABORATION • 5 COMMUNICATE WITH VISUAL LITERACY • DISNEY PARK EXPERIENCE • 6 AVOID OVE
YOUR AUDIENCE • STORY • 2 WEAR YOUR GUESTS' SHOES • PASSION • 3 ORGANIZE THE FLOW OF PEOPLE A
Y • TAKE A CHANCE / THINK DIFFERENTLY • 9 FOR EVERY OUNCE OF TREATMENT, PROVIDE A TON OF TREAT •
AVOID OVERLOAD–CREATE TURN-ONS • EDUCATION–NEVER STOP LEARNING • 7 TELL ONE STORY AT A TIME
OF PEOPLE AND IDEAS • MENTOR • 4 CREATE A WIENIE (VISUAL MAGNET) • COLLABORATION • 5 COMMUN
TREAT • BECOME THE BEST • 10 KEEP IT UP (MAINTAIN IT)! • 1 KNOW YOUR AUDIENCE • STORY • 2 WEAR
A TIME • BE CURIOUS • 8 AVOID CONTRADICTIONS–MAINTAIN IDENTITY • TAKE A CHANCE / THINK DIFFERE
OMMUNICATE WITH VISUAL LITERACY • DISNEY PARK EXPERIENCE • 6 AVOID OVERLOAD–CREATE TURN-ONS
• 2 WEAR YOUR GUESTS' SHOES • PASSION • 3 ORGANIZE THE FLOW OF PEOPLE AND IDEAS • MENTOR •
NK DIFFERENTLY • 9 FOR EVERY OUNCE OF TREATMENT, PROVIDE A TON OF TREAT • BECOME THE BEST • 10 K
RN-ONS • EDUCATION–NEVER STOP LEARNING • 7 TELL ONE STORY AT A TIME • BE CURIOUS • 8 AVOID CO
NTOR • 4 CREATE A WIENIE (VISUAL MAGNET) • COLLABORATION • 5 COMMUNICATE WITH VISUAL LITERACY
• 10 KEEP IT UP (MAINTAIN IT)! • 1 KNOW YOUR AUDIENCE • STORY • 2 WEAR YOUR GUESTS' SHOES • PASS
D CONTRADICTIONS–MAINTAIN IDENTITY • TAKE A CHANCE / THINK DIFFERENTLY • 9 FOR EVERY OUNCE OF
ERACY • DISNEY PARK EXPERIENCE • 6 AVOID OVERLOAD–CREATE TURN-ONS • EDUCATION–NEVER STOP LE
S • PASSION • 3 ORGANIZE THE FLOW OF PEOPLE AND IDEAS • MENTOR • 4 CREATE A WIENIE (VISUAL MA
OUNCE OF TREATMENT, PROVIDE A TON OF TREAT • BECOME THE BEST • 10 KEEP IT UP (MAINTAIN IT)! • 1

# ACKNOWLEDGMENTS

As the dedication for this book indicates, I owe a great debt to the Imagineers—past and present. Walt Disney created the Imagineering organization, then called WED Enterprises (for Walter Elias Disney), in 1952 to work with him in creating Disneyland. Over its sixty-some-year history, the Imagineers have become one of the world's most admired design teams, responsible for the creation and construction of all eleven Disney parks, and their complementary resorts, on three continents around the world. Literally billions of people have experienced the fun and entertainment magic that have come from the Imagineers' drawing boards during those six decades.

Through this book, it's a great thrill for me to serve as a bridge between my mentors—the original team assembled by Walt himself—and today's Imagineers, many of them part of the team I had the privilege of leading as president and then as vice chairman and principal creative executive.

I'm excited to open the doors to this very special group of talents in *One Little Spark!* through the words, thoughts, experiences, and sage advice of seventy-five Imagineers—and me, of course! Whether you are an Imagineer wannabe yourself, or a parent, grandparent, or friend interested in advising a very special talent, I know you will find this book a valuable source of inspiration and motivation.

I am also indebted to the people who played key roles in making this book a reality. That list starts with my favorite Disney Editions editor, Wendy Lefkon, editorial director for special projects. As always, the support I receive from Wendy and her staff (especially the great enthusiasm and design talent of Winnie Ho) is first class—as is the enthusiasm of my agent, Richard Curtis. And Patti Newton's two terrific maps should lead future Imagineers right to the front door!

Special thanks belong to two people whose advice and suggestions were truly "the glue" that brought this book together: my wife, Leah, and my "Sklar Editor," daughter Leslie. She is a tough mark—especially for her father. But in truth, Leslie's talent and insistence on editorial excellence and quality—and accuracy!—were among the most important influences on the outcome of this book. It is with respect and appreciation that she earned the credit "Edited by Leslie Sklar."

I also owe a great big thank you to Richard Sherman. He is a "living legacy" to me—a Disney Legend legacy, of course. It's the second time Richard has written an introduction for one of my books. I am very honored to enjoy his trust. And Glen Keane and I enjoy a "mutual admiration" relationship. His letter, written after reading my *Dream It! Do It!* book, helped motivate me to write this new manuscript.

About the book's title: With Wendy's encouragement, I wanted to send a message to my former Imagineering colleagues. For many years, I have been championing a battle cry related to Disney park entertainment: *"More songs!"* I'm a big believer, and I'll tell you why. When you think of Disney entertainment, especially motion pictures, but also television, Disney park shows, and of course the Broadway theater, your first "image" is not visual at all: it's *aural—a song*!

To prove my point, in the following I have paired songs from Disney and Pixar films just to show that *you don't need movie titles or photos of the key characters to know what the Disney story is—you just need to hear a song:* "You've Got a Friend in Me" or "I Wanna Be Like You." "Kiss the Girl" or "Can You Feel the Love Tonight." "Just Around the Riverbend" or "A Whole New World." "I Just Can't Wait to Be King" or "He's a Tramp." "I've Got No Strings" or "Let It Go." "Give a Little Whistle" or "Whistle While You Work." "Beauty and the Beast" or "Some Day My Prince Will Come." "When Somebody Loved Me" or "Baby Mine." Or the Richard and Robert Sherman tune that defies pairing (and spelling): "Supercalifragilisticexpialidocious"!

Many of these songs have played a key role in the ride-through attractions and live theatrical shows at the Disney parks. My belief is that more *original* songs should be created. Think of the legacy of original story songs in the Disney parks: "There's a Great Big Beautiful Tomorrow" from the Carousel of Progress; "it's a small world"; "Yo Ho (A Pirate's Life for Me)" from Pirates of the Caribbean; "Grim Grinning Ghosts" from The Haunted Mansion; "Golden Dreams" from Epcot's American Adventure; "Listen to the Land" from The

Land pavilion; and especially Dick and Bob Sherman's "One Little Spark" from Journey into Imagination in Epcot.

So that's how *One Little Spark!* became the main title of this book. As those simple words suggest, my goal is to offer young talent insight into the world of Imagineering as Imagineers have lived it and practiced it. And not only for future Imagineers; there is advice here for anyone with a creative bent—creative talent of today speaking to passionate young talent of tomorrow. The words to that song say it directly: all of us hope that this book will contribute to realizing *your dream,* so that it *"can be a dream come true, with just that spark, from me to you!"*

To Richard and Robert and all the great songwriters since Mickey first tooted that whistle in *Steamboat Willie* in 1928, I acknowledge you. I thank you. I can't wait for that next great Disney story that reaches my ears long before my eyes—and continues to tell the tale long after the screen has turned dark and the ride-through adventure has ended.

# CONTENTS

# INTRODUCTION
# by Richard M. Sherman

*The musical magic created by Richard M. and Robert B. Sherman for motion pictures, the stage, and Disney parks worldwide is a national treasure—recognized as such when President George W. Bush presented Dick and Bob with the National Medal of Arts in 2008 at the White House. Their music and songs have been nominated for nine Academy Awards; their compositions for Mary Poppins won Oscars for Best Original Score and Best Song ("Chim Chim Cher-ee"). Working with the Imagineers, Dick and Bob wrote Disney park theme songs for the Carousel of Progress ("There's a Great Big Beautiful Tomorrow"), "it's a small world," the Enchanted Tiki Room, and Epcot's Journey into Imagination.*

\* \* \* \* \* \* \* \* \* \*

When Marty Sklar called my brother, Robert, and me asking us to collaborate with Disney Imagineers on a project for Epcot, little did we know that we would be embarking on an exciting journey into the world of imagination. In fact, not coincidentally, the pavilion we worked on was called Journey into Imagination.

After more than thirty years, two of the three songs we wrote for that fabulous experience are no longer in use. However, I still hear from Disney fans about how much they enjoyed and how well they remember those songs. One, "Magic Journeys" (which Marty told us was his favorite), was the linking musical/lyrical theme of an ingenious 3-D film of the same name. The second, called "Makin' Memories," was for the pavilion's sponsor, Kodak. It told of the wondrous memories we can preserve by taking photographs.

However, by far my favorite was the third song. We called it "One Little Spark," and it is still playing every day at Epcot. Before Bob and I started dreaming up ideas for this one, the Imagineers showed us sketches and models of the principal characters for the show. To us, the star was Figment, a little purple dragon with "two tiny wings" and "eyes big and yellow." With just one look at that delightful character, our sparks of imagination flew, and we were off and running. It is very gratifying to know that little Figment has captured the imagination of so many millions of Epcot visitors over the years.

Therefore, when Marty asked me to introduce "One Little Spark" in his new book about the Imagineers, I was thrilled. Years ago, soon after we first wrote it, Marty told us that he felt this song was truly the theme song of Walt Disney Imagineering. What a wonderful compliment! What one little figment of imagination can start . . .

**Richard M. Sherman**
Composer/Lyricist

# One Little Spark

**Richard M. and Robert B. Sherman**

*One Little Spark*
*Of inspiration*
*Is at the heart*
*Of all creation*
*Right at the start of everything that's new*
*One little spark*
*Lights up for you*

*Imagination*
*Imagination*
*A dream can be a dream come true*
*With just that spark*
*From me to you!*

*One bright idea*
*One right connection*
*Can give our lives*
*A new direction*
*So many times we're stumbling in*
*    the dark*
*And then "Eureka!"*
*That little spark!*

*Imagination*
*Imagination*
*A dream can be a dream come true*
*With just that spark*
*From me and you!*

*One Little Spark*
*One flight of fancy*
*Shines up the dark*
*So that we can see*
*When things look grim and nothing's*
    *going right*
*One little spark*
*Clicks on the light!*

*Imagination*
*Imagination*
*A dream can be a dream come true*
*With just that spark*
*From me to you*

*Two tiny wings*
*Eyes big and yellow*
*Horns of a steer*
*But a loveable fellow*
*From head to tail he's a royal purple*
    *pigment*
*And then "voilà!"*
*You've got a Figment*

*Imagination*
*Imagination*
*A dream can be a dream come true*
*With just that spark*
*From me and you!*

# INTRODUCTION
# by Glen Keane

*Glen Keane describes himself as an "artist who animates" . . . an "actor with a pencil." For nearly four decades at Disney, Glen's signature skills created leading animated characters: Ariel, Beast, Aladdin, Tarzan. In 2007, Glen received the animation industry's highest honor, the Winsor McCay Award, "for lifetime contributions to the field of animation." His highly acclaimed experimental film Duet, created for Google, is an interactive short that explores virtual worlds by combining hand-drawn art and computer gigabytes. The following is a letter Glen sent me after reading my memoir, Dream It! Do It!*

Dear Marty,

We just flew together on Air France to Paris—at least it felt like we did because I had the joy of reading *Dream It! Do It!* I received a copy when you and I spoke to the Nike folks at the Grand Californian a few weeks back and took it with me for the long voyage. I finished it when I landed—fastest LA to Paris trip I've ever taken.

You spoke with such humor, authority, and frankness. I learned so much and now wish you had written the book 30 years ago—I may have been tempted to jump ship from Feature Animation and play in the amazing sandbox of Imagineering that you have inspired and led for so long.

I particularly enjoyed your stories of Walt Disney. I only knew him through the eyes of the 9 old men—now I have a much clearer vision of the man. Your anecdote of Walt asking Herb Ryman to come up with a concept for Disneyland in one weekend was priceless.

Even more interesting was the contrast I saw between you and Walt—his reticence for compliments and praise and your natural gift of encouragement. I saw how others who were influenced by him took on the same style of leadership—rarely giving compliments. Though I never had the honor of working directly for you, I gleaned from afar your love of people and skill in how to get the best from them by giving clear challenges and positive encouragement. Throughout your book I enjoyed how you always shined a light on the talents of others.

Thank you for all you have done at Disney and doing it in your Marty Sklar style. I'm so glad you took the time to write it down.

With deepest appreciation—

Glen

**Glen Keane,**
Animator/Glen Keane Productions

# FOREWORD:
# A Word from Marty

I did not start out writing this book to celebrate the sixtieth anniversary of Disneyland. But it's hard to avoid an event of such worldwide significance. What Walt Disney began in Anaheim, California, on July 17, 1955, has spread around the world—bringing entertainment, knowledge, and family fun to *billions* of guests on three continents, with more to come early in 2016 with the opening of the twelfth Disney park, Shanghai Disneyland.

So despite the fact that I was there in Anaheim on that July day—and that I am the only Disney cast member who has participated in the opening of all eleven parks now operating—this book was really motivated by an event that took place in Florida more than three decades ago.

With the opening of Epcot—the third of those eleven Disney parks—at Walt Disney World in October 1982, I began to receive a steady stream of requests to talk about "how Disney does it." The telephone calls and letters came from major corporations, conventions, industry groups, and university professors who wanted their employees, convention attendees, or students to learn the how-tos—the secrets of our success—from the creative talents of Walt Disney Imagineering.

At the time, I had spent eight of my eventual fifty-four years at Disney leading the Imagineers in developing the concepts, playing a key role in convincing the major corporate sponsors to make Epcot a reality, and producing the myriad shows and stories that attracted more than ten million people to visit Epcot in its first year. Naturally, I was excited to receive so many requests to represent the Imagineers at so many important venues.

My first challenge was this: how could I boil down to a few principles those eight years—indeed, the key lessons I had learned from Walt Disney and the many Disney Legends who influenced me throughout the nearly two decades I had already spent at Disneyland and Imagineering? That's when I developed the original Mickey's Ten Commandments for two speeches in 1983: one was in Minneapolis–Saint Paul to the national Convention of Science and Technology Centers, and the other was in Boston to that city's Art Directors Club.

Mickey's Ten Commandments was a hit with audiences outside and inside The Walt Disney Company from the start. *Funworld* magazine, which is published by the International Association of Amusement Parks and Attractions (IAAPA), called it "a classic—perhaps the industry's best guide to the creation of themed entertainment."

When I originally began thinking about writing a book

about Mickey's Ten Commandments, my thought was to concentrate on the commandments as the whole subject, especially as they had expanded over time beyond the original ten to encompass forty key principles. But as I traveled the country during the last two years promoting my memoir, *Dream It! Do It! My Half-Century Creating Disney's Magic Kingdoms*, published by Disney Editions in August 2013 (and now in its third printing, with a Japanese edition released and a Chinese version to follow), I realized that there was a much bigger story to tell. And *telling stories* was the key!

Those journeys were a remarkable revelation to me— even after countless experiences around the world for Walt Disney Imagineering and The Walt Disney Company. The audiences were so friendly, so anxious to know more inside stories about Walt and the Imagineers. Even my hosts were frequently surprised at the turnouts and the sales figures: seven hundred people at Chicago's Museum of Science and Industry; three hundred at the Ocean County Library in Toms River, in southern New Jersey; five hundred books sold during my appearance at Troy Carlson's Stage Nine Entertainment Store in Old Sacramento, in California; turn-away crowds and sold-out book supplies at The Walt Disney Family Museum in San Francisco and the Skirball Cultural Center in Los Angeles; and the throngs awaiting me at the book's debut at the 2013 D23 Disney fan expo at the Anaheim Convention Center.

At every stop from Seattle to Orlando, I took the time at the end of each talk for a question-and-answer session and the popular book signing that followed. It was during these signing sessions that my ideas about another book really began to take shape. Everywhere everyone wanted to hear more stories: "Was Walt really that inspiring?" "How did you create a theme park out of Walt's ideas for a community called EPCOT?" "What was it like to stand on empty land in Florida, Tokyo, Paris, and Hong Kong before the first shovelful of dirt had been moved on the site? And to stand there now next to an imposing castle and surrounded by Disney characters and thousands of guests enjoying the parks?"

And most of all in recent times: "How do I become an Imagineer?"

Sixteen-year-old Jacob Kelley from Cleveland was a classic case. His mother and father and three siblings had made a six-hour drive from their hometown to Chicago's Museum of Science and Industry *that morning* to see my presentation. And they were then driving right back as soon as Jacob, who was first in line, had his book signed. Before the talk even began, Jacob shadowed me and my host, Kurt Haunfelner, the museum's vice president of collections and exhibits, as we toured the place. He jumped in with questions at every opportunity.

And then there was the couple who wanted me to know that when they learned the night before that I would be signing books at Downtown Disney in Florida, they drove the next day all the way from Kentucky to Orlando to get an autographed copy! How far was that? I asked. The reply: it was 1,800 miles. One way!

Something was going on here that at first I did not comprehend. These were not fanatics from Kentucky blindly embarking on a quest, or parents taking their kids for a Sunday drive from Cleveland, Ohio, to Chicago, Illinois. No—these were parents and kids, and grandmas and grandpas—Disney fans who wanted me to know how much they appreciate the joy and fun and entertainment Disney has given them, how much they loved the new Cars Land at Disney California Adventure or Belle and the Beast at the Be Our Guest Restaurant in the new Fantasyland at Walt Disney World's Magic Kingdom. They wanted to know *everything about everything*—how we created it, what Walt and Roy Disney were *really* like. Others wanted to know if we were going to do a *Frozen* show—and again and again, "How can Henry and Penelope become Imagineers?"

I finally got the message. Yes—tell us about your Mickey's Ten Commandments, but also tell us more stories, and then answer this question: "What should Owen and Alice and Lucy and Eli and Jake and Rachel do to prepare for a career designing Disney parks and resorts as an Imagineer?"

So, that's the idea for this book: to communicate the principles my career was built on and to direct you to The Road to Imagineering.

OMMUNICATE WITH VISUAL LITERACY • DISNEY PARK EXPERIENCE • 6 AVOID OVERLOAD—CREATE TURN-ONS
• 2 WEAR YOUR GUESTS' SHOES • PASSION • 3 ORGANIZE THE FLOW OF PEOPLE AND IDEAS • MENTOR •
K DIFFERENTLY • 9 FOR EVERY OUNCE OF TREATMENT, PROVIDE A TON OF TREAT • BECOME THE BEST • 10 K
N-ONS • EDUCATION—NEVER STOP LEARNING • 7 TELL ONE STORY AT A TIME • BE CURIOUS • 8 AVOID CO
TOR • 4 CREATE A WIENIE (VISUAL MAGNET) • COLLABORATION • 5 COMMUNICATE WITH VISUAL LITERACY
• 10 KEEP IT UP (MAINTAIN IT)! • 1 KNOW YOUR AUDIENCE • STORY • 2 WEAR YOUR GUESTS' SHOES • PASS
CONTRADICTIONS—MAINTAIN IDENTITY • TAKE A CHANCE / THINK DIFFERENTLY • 9 FOR EVERY OUNCE OF
RACY • DISNEY PARK EXPERIENCE • 6 AVOID OVERLOAD—CREATE TURN-ONS • EDUCATION—NEVER STOP LE
S • PASSION • 3 ORGANIZE THE FLOW OF PEOPLE AND IDEAS • MENTOR • 4 CREATE A WIENIE (VISUAL MA
OUNCE OF TREATMENT, PROVIDE A TON OF TREAT • BECOME THE BEST • 10 KEEP IT UP (MAINTAIN IT)! • 1
VER STOP LEARNING • 7 TELL ONE STORY AT A TIME • BE CURIOUS • 8 AVOID CONTRADICTIONS—MAINTAI
IE (VISUAL MAGNET) • COLLABORATION • 5 COMMUNICATE WITH VISUAL LITERACY • DISNEY PARK EXPERI
NTAIN IT)! • 1 KNOW YOUR AUDIENCE • STORY • 2 WEAR YOUR GUESTS' SHOES • PASSION • 3 ORGANIZ
TIONS—MAINTAIN IDENTITY • TAKE A CHANCE / THINK DIFFERENTLY • 9 FOR EVERY OUNCE OF TREATMENT,
EY PARK EXPERIENCE • 6 AVOID OVERLOAD—CREATE TURN-ONS • EDUCATION—NEVER STOP LEARNING • 7
N • 3 ORGANIZE THE FLOW OF PEOPLE AND IDEAS • MENTOR • 4 CREATE A WIENIE (VISUAL MAGNET) • CO
REATMENT, PROVIDE A TON OF TREAT • BECOME THE BEST • 10 KEEP IT UP (MAINTAIN IT)! • 1 KNOW YOUR A
NG • 7 TELL ONE STORY AT A TIME • BE CURIOUS • 8 AVOID CONTRADICTIONS—MAINTAIN IDENTITY • TAKE
T) • COLLABORATION • 5 COMMUNICATE WITH VISUAL LITERACY • DISNEY PARK EXPERIENCE • 6 AVOID OV
YOUR AUDIENCE • STORY • 2 WEAR YOUR GUESTS' SHOES • PASSION • 3 ORGANIZE THE FLOW OF PEOPLE
• TAKE A CHANCE / THINK DIFFERENTLY • 9 FOR EVERY OUNCE OF TREATMENT, PROVIDE A TON OF TREAT •
VOID OVERLOAD—CREATE TURN-ONS • EDUCATION—NEVER STOP LEARNING • 7 TELL ONE STORY AT A TIME
OF PEOPLE AND IDEAS • MENTOR • 4 CREATE A WIENIE (VISUAL MAGNET) • COLLABORATION • 5 COMMUN
TREAT • BECOME THE BEST • 10 KEEP IT UP (MAINTAIN IT)! • 1 KNOW YOUR AUDIENCE • STORY • 2 WEAR
TIME • BE CURIOUS • 8 AVOID CONTRADICTIONS—MAINTAIN IDENTITY • TAKE A CHANCE / THINK DIFFERE
OMMUNICATE WITH VISUAL LITERACY • DISNEY PARK EXPERIENCE • 6 AVOID OVERLOAD—CREATE TURN-ONS
• 2 WEAR YOUR GUESTS' SHOES • PASSION • 3 ORGANIZE THE FLOW OF PEOPLE AND IDEAS • MENTOR •
K DIFFERENTLY • 9 FOR EVERY OUNCE OF TREATMENT, PROVIDE A TON OF TREAT • BECOME THE BEST • 10 K
N-ONS • EDUCATION—NEVER STOP LEARNING • 7 TELL ONE STORY AT A TIME • BE CURIOUS • 8 AVOID CO
TOR • 4 CREATE A WIENIE (VISUAL MAGNET) • COLLABORATION • 5 COMMUNICATE WITH VISUAL LITERACY
• 10 KEEP IT UP (MAINTAIN IT)! • 1 KNOW YOUR AUDIENCE • STORY • 2 WEAR YOUR GUESTS' SHOES • PASS
CONTRADICTIONS—MAINTAIN IDENTITY • TAKE A CHANCE / THINK DIFFERENTLY • 9 FOR EVERY OUNCE OF
RACY • DISNEY PARK EXPERIENCE • 6 AVOID OVERLOAD—CREATE TURN-ONS • EDUCATION—NEVER STOP LE
S • PASSION • 3 ORGANIZE THE FLOW OF PEOPLE AND IDEAS • MENTOR • 4 CREATE A WIENIE (VISUAL MA
OUNCE OF TREATMENT, PROVIDE A TON OF TREAT • BECOME THE BEST • 10 KEEP IT UP (MAINTAIN IT)!

# One Little Spark!

## Mickey's Ten Commandments and **The Road to Imagineering**

E CO
MUNICATE
ORY • 2 WEAR YOUR
ANCE / THINK DIFFERENTLY •
VERLOAD—CREATE TURN-ONS • EDUC
PEOPLE AND IDEAS • MENTOR • 4 CREATE A
A TON OF TREAT • BECOME THE BEST • 10 KEEP IT U
TH ONE STORY AT A TIME • BE CURIOUS • 8 AVOID CONTRA

CE OF TREATMENT, PROVIDE A TON OF TREAT
STOP LEARNING • I TELL ONE STORY
SUAL MAGNET) • COLLABORA
) • I KNOW YOUR
AIN IDENTIT
ENP

WEAR YOUR GUESTS SHOES · PASSION · 3 ORGANIZ
TY · 9 FOR EVERY OUNCE OF TREATMENT, PRI
ON—NEVER STOP LEARNING · 7 TELI
UAL MAGNET) · COLLABOR
KNOW YOUR AUDIE
TAKE A CH
C

# DON'T AVOID
# THE CLICHÉS

When I began assembling Mickey's Ten Commandments, I quickly realized how many shoulders I was standing on. Many of my colleagues at Walt Disney Imagineering were veterans of thirty or even forty years at Disney—and the lessons they served up every day offered the equivalent of a graduate degree in design and storytelling.

The list of Imagineers who became my mentors is a who's who of Disney animation, film, and park design—Disney Legends all. There was John Hench, who joined Disney in 1939 to work on *Fantasia* and, after a remarkable career creating background environments for animated films, grew into Walt's favorite park "place maker." Along the way, Hench designed Space Mountain and Epcot's Spaceship Earth.

Herbert Dickens Ryman graduated from the Art Institute of Chicago in 1932 and came to Disney after making his mark as a story sketch artist in the heyday of MGM and Twentieth Century-Fox, where his illustrations helped set the look of *David Copperfield, Mutiny on the Bounty,* and *Anna and the King of Siam.*

At Imagineering, he created some of the most famous placemaking illustrations in the world, including the first overall drawing of Disneyland and the castles of Disneyland and Walt Disney World.

Another, Marc Davis, was a pillar in Disney animation. He was one of the Nine Old Men—Walt's famous circle of his most brilliant animation stars. Marc came to Imagineering after more than twenty-five years creating some of Disney's most memorable female characters in animated films, including Tinker Bell, Cruella De Vil, and both Aurora and Maleficent in *Sleeping Beauty.* For the parks, Marc created pirates, ghosts, talking tiki poles, and bathing jungle elephants.

There was also Harper Goff, designer of the *Nautilus* submarine for *20,000 Leagues Under the Sea* and (outside Disney) art director for 1971's *Willy Wonka & the Chocolate Factory* and production designer for 1958's *The Vikings.*

I can easily name a dozen more who taught me A to Z in storytelling, design, and communication—every one a master at his craft—including the first female Imagineer, Harriet Burns. She was queen of the Model Shop, where sketches by Ryman and Hench and Davis and Goff were turned into three-dimensional design studies by Fred Joerger, Claude Coats, and Rolly Crump. Harriet was Walt's favorite; she was the petite Texan with exquisite taste and talent who could sling it with all the boys.

Members of this amazing group of talents were my mentors, my friends, and—when I became the creative leader of

Imagineering—my staff. They were the best of the best. They defined "Imagineer" and "Imagineering." Their dedication to Walt, and their comprehension of his passion for excellence, knew no bounds. They were true believers, followers, and teachers. Walt created Imagineering, but the talent he brought together made pirates fight and ghosts dance.

Of course, it was Walt Disney who set the direction from the beginning. Working from a script I wrote, here is how Walt put it during the presentation when he and his brother Roy announced the Walt Disney World project in Orlando in November 1965:

> *We keep moving forward, opening up new doors, because we're curious. . . . We're always exploring and experimenting. We have never lost our faith in family entertainment—stories that make people laugh, stories about warm and human things. . . . We're not out to make a fast dollar with gimmicks. We're interested in doing things that are fun—in bringing pleasure and especially laughter to people. And probably most important of all, when we consider a new project we really study it—not just the surface idea but everything about it! And when we go into that new project, we believe in it all the way. We have confidence in our ability to do it right. And we work hard to do the best possible job!*

\* \* \* \* \* \* \* \* \* \*

I've often thought about what those Disney Legends brought to the new medium of storytelling that Walt Disney created with Disneyland. That is why I enlisted seventy-five current and former Imagineers to join me in bringing this Imagineering story into the twenty-first century—it's more than sixty years since Walt founded Imagineering as WED Enterprises (an acronym formed by the initials of Walter Elias Disney) in 1952. Times have changed—but basic Disney principles have remained steadfast and relevant through the years.

The roots of Mickey's Ten Commandments came from the inspiration and teachings of those great Imagineers—and from a host of amazing talents we had the good fortune to work with or simply meet and share ideas with. Some of my fondest memories are of the projects and times we spent working with talent from outside the Imagineering roster.

The great science fiction writer Ray Bradbury—author of *The Martian Chronicles* and *Fahrenheit 451*—helped us define the story of communication in Epcot's Spaceship Earth. Don Hewitt, creator and producer of CBS's *60 Minutes*, discussed Epcot concepts and explained that his direction to *60 Minutes* reporters was inspired by the Bible: "Tell me a story!" Don instructed.

And a London-born theater man named Shaike Weinberg, who had created The Jewish Diaspora Museum in Tel Aviv, Israel, and later became the founding director of the United States Holocaust Memorial Museum in Washington, D.C., had this to say: "The great museums not only show you [artifacts], but also tell you a story!"

Of course, we also turned to the modern-day master of storytelling magic, John Lasseter, who with partners Ed Catmull and Steve Jobs created Pixar, giving life to some of our most beloved stories and characters: Woody and Buzz Lightyear of *Toy Story*, Nemo and Dory of *Finding Nemo*,

Sulley and Mike of *Monsters, Inc.*, and of course Lightning McQueen and Mater of *Cars*.

We've all heard the cliché "out of the mouths of babes"—meaning that often "pearls of wisdom" come from the youngest among us. But more likely, the pearls we treasure at Imagineering came from the great talents we worked with on projects for the Disney parks—and often it was a simple statement in the course of a meeting or discussion that became memorable. Three of my favorites come immediately to mind:

> **"Don't avoid the clichés—they are clichés because they work!"**
>
> George Lucas, motion picture and
> television director, writer, producer

We were meeting at the Imagineering offices in 1985 to discuss the Star Tours simulator attraction. The charge was to find a way to interpret George Lucas's *Star Wars* films in a four-and-a-half-minute experience. It was all new to all of us—it was the first simulator show of its kind when it opened little more than a year after concept work began. One of my colleagues complained about the number of clichés that seemed to flow from our Imagineering team members. That's when George Lucas spoke up with the sage advice: "Don't avoid the clichés—they are clichés because they work!"

> **"Our guests don't go out of the parks whistling the lights or the architecture."**
>
> John Hench, designer extraordinaire
> and Disney Legend

John Hench was our philosopher-king, friend of Salvador Dalí, world traveler, and a walking encyclopedia of knowledge. A concept meeting for the American Adventure show at Epcot was in progress at one point, with designers striving to improve elements of the project. We had a spectacular finale that some of the designers thought was over the top—too complex and too expensive. John grew more and more irritated as the argument raged on about what would be "good enough."

Hench knew there were budgetary and scheduling issues. But during his sixty-four-year career at Disney, he learned that the key reason attractions like Disneyland's Enchanted Tiki Room and the Adventureland Jungle Cruise are still entertaining guests more than half a century after their debuts is that no one settled for "good enough" in the design phase. Finally, John spoke up: "Our guests don't go out of the parks whistling the lights or the architecture!" We put that finale with the "cherry and whipped cream on top" back in the show. How? We created two additional figures of our hosts, Ben Franklin and Mark Twain, gave them a towering dimensional Statue of Liberty in the background, set off a huge fireworks display all around them in New York Harbor, and called it a curtain call!

> **"Poor taste costs no more!"**
> Herb Ryman, artist, illustrator, and Disney Legend

Herb Ryman was arguably the greatest illustrator in the history of the attractions business. Walt Disney entrusted him to create the most important illustrations in Disney park history—including the very first overall depictions of

Disneyland Park, Walt Disney World, and Epcot. Herb had a way of succinctly capturing the essence of a concept or issue—and letting you and everyone else know exactly how he felt. I don't recall the specific project, but I vividly recall Herb's reaction to it: "Poor taste costs no more," he cautioned us. If that critique didn't get our attention, Ryman's explanation did: if you build something that's poorly thought out and designed, chances are it will cost just about as much as a well-thought-out, beautifully designed project.

Herb wanted to be sure that whatever we did, we should design and build it *the best possible way*. He wanted us to be able to say, "I did the best I know how," or, as Walt Disney said, "Work hard to do the best possible job!"

* * * * * * * * * *

Yes, there were great philosophers on our early Imagineering teams—just as there are today. Yet no understanding of the Imagineers and their successes around the world is possible without recognizing that the achievements of the Imagineers are not those of brilliant individuals acting alone—it's all about the perfect blending of talents. In a word, it's teamwork.

When I first became a full-time Imagineer in 1961, John Hench pulled me aside and provided the wisdom that became the touchstone throughout my entire career: "When we open a new attraction or whole park, you can't say, '*I* did this,' or, '*I* did that,' because so many talented hands have touched it. It's a '*we* business'—not an '*I* business'!"

Years after that early lesson, Warren Bennis, distinguished professor of business administration at the University of Southern California's Marshall School of Business, spoke at Imagineering. I was impressed by what he had to say and afterward sought out his book *Organizing Genius: The Secrets of Creative Collaboration*, cowritten with Patricia Ward Biederman. As soon as I read the title page, I knew he was a kindred spirit. Professor Bennis's opening line reads "None of us is as smart as all of us."

As obvious as that sounds, it is *not* standard practice in most of our life experiences. The "star system" rules so many aspects of our world, but nowhere is it more obvious than in the entertainment business.

In the movie business, individual recognition is written into performance contracts: a star's name must appear as a percentage of the size of the film's title; there's a pecking order of names on the film credits (above or below the title—to be negotiated); a "*my* trailer is bigger than *yours*" mentality; special transportation to and from the shooting site is mandatory; and "I'll do *this* project if you commit to starring me in your *next* project!" Those are all "I business" standards.

In contrast, a "we business" creates an environment where *all* the talent is celebrated together—artists, writers, designers, engineers, architects, landscapers, computer technicians, graphic artists, etc. At Imagineering, that encompasses 140 different disciplines. We believe strongly in Professor Bennis's axiom: "None of us is as smart as all of us." (Professor Bennis passed away in 2013, but his wisdom and lessons live on.)

The blending of so many talented people into one great creative force is the story of this book. For most Imagineers, the Road to Imagineering has many twists and turns—both anticipated and completely surprising. It's my great hope that when you get to the end of the book, you will remember one of the most important lessons I learned about leadership from Walt Disney: don't pigeonhole anybody! You never know what talented people can do if you give them a chance—if *they* are willing to *take a chance*. It's exactly what so many Imagineers have done on The Road to Imagineering.

Ready? It's time to start your journey. I hope this book inspires you to learn and grow—no matter what you have chosen or will choose as your life's work. And if it happens to include creating family entertainment for billions of people around the world, as it did for me, always remember to give back. Because, as Walt Disney taught us, you don't do it for yourself.

\* \* \* \* \* \* \* \* \* \*

OMMUNICATE WITH VISUAL LITERACY • DISNEY PARK EXPERIENCE • 6 AVOID OVERLOAD—CREATE TURN-O
• 2 WEAR YOUR GUESTS' SHOES • PASSION • 3 ORGANIZE THE FLOW OF PEOPLE AND IDEAS • MENTOR
NK DIFFERENTLY • 9 FOR EVERY OUNCE OF TREATMENT, PROVIDE A TON OF TREAT • BECOME THE BEST • 10
RN-ONS • EDUCATION—NEVER STOP LEARNING • 7 TELL ONE STORY AT A TIME • BE CURIOUS • 8 AVOID C
NTOR • 4 CREATE A WIENIE (VISUAL MAGNET) • COLLABORATION • 5 COMMUNICATE WITH VISUAL LITERAC
• 10 KEEP IT UP (MAINTAIN IT)! • 1 KNOW YOUR AUDIENCE • STORY • 2 WEAR YOUR GUESTS' SHOES • PAS
D CONTRADICTIONS—MAINTAIN IDENTITY • TAKE A CHANCE / THINK DIFFERENTLY • 9 FOR EVERY OUNCE O
ERACY • DISNEY PARK EXPERIENCE • 6 AVOID OVERLOAD—CREATE TURN-ONS • EDUCATION—NEVER STOP L
S • PASSION • 3 ORGANIZE THE FLOW OF PEOPLE AND IDEAS • MENTOR • 4 CREATE A WIENIE (VISUAL M.
OUNCE OF TREATMENT, PROVIDE A TON OF TREAT • BECOME THE BEST • 10 KEEP IT UP (MAINTAIN IT)! •
EVER STOP LEARNING • 7 TELL ONE STORY AT A TIME • BE CURIOUS • 8 AVOID CONTRADICTIONS—MAINTA
NIE (VISUAL MAGNET) • COLLABORATION • 5 COMMUNICATE WITH VISUAL LITERACY • DISNEY PARK EXPEI
AINTAIN IT)! • 1 KNOW YOUR AUDIENCE • STORY • 2 WEAR YOUR GUESTS' SHOES • PASSION • 3 ORGANI
TIONS—MAINTAIN IDENTITY • TAKE A CHANCE / THINK DIFFERENTLY • 9 FOR EVERY OUNCE OF TREATMENT,
NEY PARK EXPERIENCE • 6 AVOID OVERLOAD—CREATE TURN-ONS • EDUCATION—NEVER STOP LEARNING •
N • 3 ORGANIZE THE FLOW OF PEOPLE AND IDEAS • MENTOR • 4 CREATE A WIENIE (VISUAL MAGNET) • C
REATMENT, PROVIDE A TON OF TREAT • BECOME THE BEST • 10 KEEP IT UP (MAINTAIN IT)! • 1 KNOW YOUR
ING • 7 TELL ONE STORY AT A TIME • BE CURIOUS • 8 AVOID CONTRADICTIONS—MAINTAIN IDENTITY • TAK
T) • COLLABORATION • 5 COMMUNICATE WITH VISUAL LITERACY • DISNEY PARK EXPERIENCE • 6 AVOID OV
YOUR AUDIENCE • STORY • 2 WEAR YOUR GUESTS' SHOES • PASSION • 3 ORGANIZE THE FLOW OF PEOPLE
Y • TAKE A CHANCE / THINK DIFFERENTLY • 9 FOR EVERY OUNCE OF TREATMENT, PROVIDE A TON OF TREAT
AVOID OVERLOAD—CREATE TURN-ONS • EDUCATION—NEVER STOP LEARNING • 7 TELL ONE STORY AT A TIM
OF PEOPLE AND IDEAS • MENTOR • 4 CREATE A WIENIE (VISUAL MAGNET) • COLLABORATION • 5 COMMUN
TREAT • BECOME THE BEST • 10 KEEP IT UP (MAINTAIN IT)! • 1 KNOW YOUR AUDIENCE • STORY • 2 WEAI
TIME • BE CURIOUS • 8 AVOID CONTRADICTIONS—MAINTAIN IDENTITY • TAKE A CHANCE / THINK DIFFERE
OMMUNICATE WITH VISUAL LITERACY • DISNEY PARK EXPERIENCE • 6 AVOID OVERLOAD—CREATE TURN-ON
• 2 WEAR YOUR GUESTS' SHOES • PASSION • 3 ORGANIZE THE FLOW OF PEOPLE AND IDEAS • MENTOR •
NK DIFFERENTLY • 9 FOR EVERY OUNCE OF TREATMENT, PROVIDE A TON OF TREAT • BECOME THE BEST • 10 I
RN-ONS • EDUCATION—NEVER STOP LEARNING • 7 TELL ONE STORY AT A TIME • BE CURIOUS • 8 AVOID CC
NTOR • 4 CREATE A WIENIE (VISUAL MAGNET) • COLLABORATION • 5 COMMUNICATE WITH VISUAL LITERAC
• 10 KEEP IT UP (MAINTAIN IT)! • 1 KNOW YOUR AUDIENCE • STORY • 2 WEAR YOUR GUESTS' SHOES • PAS
D CONTRADICTIONS—MAINTAIN IDENTITY • TAKE A CHANCE / THINK DIFFERENTLY • 9 FOR EVERY OUNCE OF
ERACY • DISNEY PARK EXPERIENCE • 6 AVOID OVERLOAD—CREATE TURN-ONS • EDUCATION—NEVER STOP L
S • PASSION • 3 ORGANIZE THE FLOW OF PEOPLE AND IDEAS • MENTOR • 4 CREATE A WIENIE (VISUAL MA
OUNCE OF TREATMENT, PROVIDE A TON OF TREAT • BECOME THE BEST • 10 KEEP IT UP (MAINTAIN IT)

WEAR YOUR GUESTS SHOES • PASSION • 3 ORGANIZI
TY • 9 FOR EVERY OUNCE OF TREATMENT, PRO
ON—NEVER STOP LEARNING • 7 TELL
IAL MAGNET) • COLLABORA
KNOW YOUR AUDIE
TAKE A CH

# MICKEY'S
# TEN COMMANDMENTS

If you were to tour Walt Disney Imagineering (sorry—tours are off-limits because the halls and walls are full of newly developed proprietary ideas), you would find the original version of Mickey's Ten Commandments on the office walls of many Imagineers. I initially wrote these to explain to and remind fellow Imagineers about the foundation principles on which our success has been built. Later I made them the centerpiece of my speeches beyond the halls of Imagineering.

For me, these principles have formed the standard the Imagineers have used to create the Disney park experiences around the world. When we followed them closely, we created magic. When we strayed from them . . . well, you will find examples of not achieving our objectives later in this book.

## 1. KNOW YOUR AUDIENCE
Identify the prime audience for your attraction or show before you begin design.

## 2. WEAR YOUR GUESTS' SHOES
Insist that your team members experience your creation just the way guests do it.

## 3. ORGANIZE THE FLOW OF PEOPLE AND IDEAS
Make sure there is a logic and sequence in your stories and in the way guests experience them.

## 4. CREATE A WIENIE (VISUAL MAGNET)
Create visual "targets" that lead visitors clearly and logically through the experience you've built.

## 5. COMMUNICATE WITH VISUAL LITERACY
Make good use of color, shape, form, texture—all the nonverbal ways of communication.

## 6. AVOID OVERLOAD—CREATE TURN-ONS
Resist the temptation to overload your audience with too much information and too many objects.

## 7. TELL ONE STORY AT A TIME
Stick to the story line; good stories are clear, logical, and consistent.

## 8. AVOID CONTRADICTIONS—MAINTAIN IDENTITY
Details in design or content that contradict one another confuse an audience about your story and its time period.

## 9. FOR EVERY OUNCE OF TREATMENT, PROVIDE A TON OF TREAT
In our business, Walt Disney said, you can educate people—but don't tell them you're doing it! Make it fun!

## 10. KEEP IT UP (MAINTAIN IT)!
In a Disney park or resort, everything must work. Poor maintenance is poor show!

EAR YOUR GUESTS SHOES · PASSION · 3 ORGANIZ
IY · 9 FOR EVERY OUNCE OF TREATMENT, PRO
ON—NEVER STOP LEARNING · 7 TELL
UAL MAGNET) · COLLABORA
KNOW YOUR AUDIE
TAKE A CH

# THE MOUSECAR
# AND THE GOOF

The entertainment industry presents its members with all sorts of awards. As much as I hate to mimic them, I'm going to do one more, with one judge and jury: me.

Many years ago, in 1947 to be exact, Walt Disney created his own version of the Oscar to honor employees or associates who made a significant contribution to the success of the company. Instead of an Oscar, Walt called the award the Mousecar. The very first recipient was Walt's brother Roy O. Disney, who was then the chairman of The Walt Disney Company.

Each of the Mickey's Ten Commandments I write about will include a story about a Disney park attraction or show or person somewhere in the world (our eleven parks are on three continents) that deserves to receive a Mousecar because it—or he or she or they—earns recognition for achievement. Remember the *team* thing!

By contrast, not every idea or attraction or person is successful, and there are always (in hindsight) reasons those concepts did not work. This is not something we hide from. So my plan is to recognize those projects, too.

Although Walt did not create this award, it seems appropriate to design an award for what we can learn in failure as well as success. So my good friend Joe Lanzisero—trained as an animator but now the vice president for Imagineering projects in Hong Kong—has designed the award for unfulfilled or underachieved projects. That award I have called The Goof!

Walt Disney once said, "I'm glad I had a good, hard failure early in my career." That failure taught Walt an important lesson, and understanding *why* he had failed led him to unprecedented achievements and honors—including thirty-two Academy Awards and the Presidential Medal of Freedom. By studying why we succeed, and how we fail, the true achievers and change makers in our world point the way to building better lives, great companies, and experiences that live on long after their own lifetimes.

On the pages that follow, I have used Mickey's Ten Commandments to illustrate the success—and failure—of projects around the world.

# COMMANDMENT #1

# KNOW YOUR AUDIENCE

I can't imagine beginning any assignment without knowing the prime audience for your story or product. How you communicate, what you communicate, is totally influenced by who you identify as your target audience.

At Disney our approach to the development of the parks was determined from the very beginning by Walt Disney. Frustrated by taking his two daughters to amusement parks where he sat alone on a bench eating popcorn while his girls rode the kiddie rides, Walt determined that there should be a park "where parents and children can have fun together."

Our audience became *the family* that does things *together*. It has remained that way, whether the family is American, Japanese, French, or Chinese—living in the countries where Disney's parks are located—and of course for families and friends from all the nations near and far who come to the Disney parks and resorts to play and learn and have fun together, young and old alike.

Clearly define your audience and you have taken the first step to achieving a successful experience, venture, or communication.

# And the Mousecar goes to . . .

## Cars Land at Disney California Adventure

I sat on a park bench with my wife, Leah, as day turned to dusk, and the neon signs began to light up along "Route 66" on opening day at Disney California Adventure's Cars Land. A seven-year-old walking past us suddenly stopped in his tracks. "Look, Mom," he yelled. "This is where they shot the movie!"

It was a well-deserved compliment for John Lasseter's Disney/Pixar 2006 *Cars* film, now come to life three-dimensionally, complete with the Cozy Cone Motel, Flo's V8 Café, and, of course, Radiator Springs Racers. Cars Land could also get a Mousecar for defining a team effort—with Imagineers Kathy Mangum (producer), Kevin Rafferty (concept and storywriter), and Zsolt Hormay (rockwork for the Cadillac Mountain Range) joining forces with Pixar's Roger Gould (concept and story), Liz Gazzano (producer), and Bill Cone (concept art) to lead this award-winning combination of talents.

How this team effort between Imagineering and Pixar came about is one of the intriguing stories about Cars Land, according to Rafferty:

In 2004—eight years before Cars Land opened—Robert Coltrin and I began work on a land inspired by California car culture. At the same time, unbeknownst to us, Pixar was working on a new movie about cars. As soon as we found out, we hopped on a plane to Pixar's headquarters in Emeryville, California, hoping there might be something in the movie that we could use in our 1950–60s-era, car-themed concept we were calling Carland.

While John Lasseter, Pixar's creative leader and the director of the Cars movie, was giving us a sneak peek at the concept art and early development reels, we fell in love with the characters, the story, and their animated world. Within six weeks of that Pixar visit, and two years before the movie was released, we had our major attraction—Radiator Springs Racers—all storyboarded. By 2007, fueled by the film's success, John suggested we change the name from Carland to Cars Land, and we realized the only way we could deliver the grandeur of Ornament Valley, the entire town of Radiator Springs, and the car characters that lived there—all elements our guests loved from the movie—was to team up with the moviemakers.

The challenge was not only to construct the iconic world portrayed in the movie; we also had to "fill in the blanks" with additional and invented stories—whole areas that were not in the film. Moviegoers didn't get to step inside Flo's V8 Café, and Stanley's Oasis did not even exist.

And then there were the "rules" Pixar established for the parallel universe where the cars lived. We stuck to the rules of the movie, even when we were *making stuff up—things not in the movie but could be!*

*There was one more key connection between Imagineering's placemaking and Pixar's storytelling. John Lasseter believes in thorough research to ensure the worlds Pixar creates are authentic. He suggested that—just as the Pixar team had done—we "get our kicks on Route 66." So we joined our Pixar partners for ten days of sketching and photo taking along the "Mother Road." The trip inspired a tremendous amount of ideas and designs for our new land— including the interiors of the buildings in the town and the kind of materials we used for the structures. And more importantly, it brought the two teams together; you might say, it made us one in "highway heaven."*

*So it's no wonder that when children step into Cars Land at Disney California Adventure, they believe that this is where the movie was filmed.*

Once the target audience—fans of the *Cars* animated feature—had been determined, the Cars Land team dedicated themselves to knowing the source material so they could meet—and exceed—the audience's expectations.

# And The Goof goes to . . .

### Meet the World in Tokyo Disneyland

Sometimes a well-intentioned idea is a disaster waiting to unfold. With Tokyo Disneyland, our first non-U.S. park venture, which opened in 1983, Disney chairman E. Cardon Walker determined it was important to show our respect for Japanese history—and to create a show that would give school administrators a logical reason for approving field trips to the park for Japanese students. Our history lesson, called Meet the World, was presented in a carousel-theater format—like the rotating theater Walt created for the General Electric Carousel of Progress at the 1964–65 New York World's Fair.

The talent we mobilized for this one was impressive: there was a title song by Richard M. and Robert B. Sherman with design by Imagineering greats Herb Ryman and Harper Goff. Yet the show foundered from the beginning—and for obvious reasons.

Bob and Dick Sherman tried to make the show's message palatable with this song:

**Meet the World**
**Richard M. and Robert B. Sherman**

*Born of the great mother sea*
*The outside world was a great mystery*
*We lived on our islands alone*
*'Til our first sailors explored the unknown*

*Reaching out, friendly hands*
*To meet the world around us*
*Friendly people of Japan*
*We meet the world with love*
*We meet the world with love*
*We meet the world with love*

*Reaching out, friendly hands*
*We meet the world with love*

*Japan of today leads the way*
*Dynamic dreams and great hopes on display*
*And each year our efforts increase*
*Touching all the world over with friendship*
*   and peace*

*Reaching out, friendly hands*
*To meet the world around us*
*Friendly people of Japan*
*We meet the world with love*
*We meet the world with love*
*We meet the world with love*
*Reaching out, friendly hands*
*We meet the world with love*

But Japanese audiences were looking for fun in Tokyo Disneyland, not a history lesson glossing over the realities of Japan's role in World War II. They may have been ready to "meet the world with love," but they did not welcome this attraction with the same feeling. Although the attraction had a sponsor that prevented its early demise, it was finally closed in 2002. It was replaced in 2009 by the immensely popular Monsters, Inc. Ride & Go Seek!

WEAR YOUR GUESTS' SHOES · PASSION · 3 ORGANIZ
TY · 9 FOR EVERY OUNCE OF TREATMENT, PR
ON—NEVER STOP LEARNING · 7 TEL
UAL MAGNET) · COLLABOR
KNOW YOUR AUDIE
TAKE A CH

# COMMANDMENT #2

# WEAR YOUR GUESTS' SHOES

Read Walter Isaacson's biography of Steve Jobs and you will understand how this commandment applies to creating any product. Jobs's focus on detail became an obsession. Beyond the devices, he spent endless time perfecting the packaging so that the entire experience of opening the box was part of the Apple magic. Understanding how your customers, guests, or audience will first experience your product is fundamental to making it something they will be drawn to and want to experience over and over again.

In the earliest days of Disneyland, when everything was new for the guests and the Imagineers, Walt Disney decreed that every designer was to go to the park at least every other week and stand in the lines (we call them queues) to understand what our guests were experiencing.

I fondly recall the script I wrote to inaugurate the

Disneyland Guided Tours ($3 for adults; $2 for kids under twelve!) in 1962. In an effort to understand the guest experience firsthand, I led the first tour myself. The second and third tours were led by Dick Nunis, director of park operations, and Jack Lindquist, the head of marketing. When we sat down afterward to review the reactions of our guests, we had input from the operators about how it functioned and the marketers about how to sell it, plus of course my own comments and revisions based on the direct reactions, observations, and timing I had experienced in leading the first Disneyland Guided Tour.

"Wear your guests' shoes" every chance you get—it's a great way to make sure you are achieving what you set out to accomplish.

# And the Mousecar goes to . . .

## Dumbo the Flying Elephant, Fantasyland— Magic Kingdom, Walt Disney World

I'm so glad that some very inventive and creative Imagineers came up with a way to overcome a mistake that I had made by insisting on the *principle* over the *practical*.

The headline in the *Orlando Sentinel* said it all: "Fantasyland's Dumbo: Old, New and Times Two at Walt Disney World." The story went on to say, "Inside the new Dumbo ride the Big Top replaces long lines with pagers and interactive games."

*Inside*, in fact, is the key word—and the magic formula.

Particularly during the summer, the long lines that formed outside the Dumbo the Flying Elephant attraction (which features sixteen pachyderm vehicles) had always been a challenge for parents with kids—and for Magic Kingdom operators dealing with one of the most popular attractions, due to its very limited capacity.

For years, the park operations team wanted to add a second Dumbo attraction—but I resisted on aesthetic grounds. Just placing sixteen more flying elephants right next to the first sixteen did not make much sense to me. Surely we Imagineers could come up with a more creative solution—that's what we do.

The renovation of Fantasyland, which opened in its new form in stages between 2012 and 2014, allowed Imagineering's creative team, led by Chris Beatty, a chance to solve the problem: it did so by creating a tentlike structure—a big top—to enclose an air-conditioned playground that would become a queue without a queue. Now each family waiting their turn is given a pager that looks like a circus ticket (it beeps when it's time to ride the elephants) and is let loose in a circus-themed playground with nets, slides, and other fun stuff that makes the young ones feel almost as if they are part of a circus performance.

Beatty gave me the full story of how the New Fantasyland team developed this elegant solution:

*Although there were numerous challenges for Imagineering's New Fantasyland team, none was as daunting as reinventing the Dumbo the Flying Elephant attraction. We knew that if we were to physically move Dumbo to a new location, we would* have to work hard to craft an entirely new story, one that placed the guest experience first.

For millions of guests each year, a visit to the Magic Kingdom is not complete without riding Dumbo the Flying Elephant. It has become a rite of passage for so many families visiting the Magic Kingdom. With an attraction of this popularity, the wait times can be very long, and the queue experience is often unbearable for some of our youngest guests. Members of our New Fantasyland team have experienced this firsthand, as many of us have small children and have waited in the midsummer heat to ride Dumbo.

During the Blue Sky process, the team quickly realized that we could transform waiting in the queue and make it fun. For us, it made sense to invite our guests inside the Big Top to enjoy the pageantry of Dumbo's Circus as they waited to ride this popular attraction. The idea excited us because we were able to extend the story over the entire guest experience by letting them play and relax in an air-conditioned, circus-themed environment.

The concept was particularly challenging because we were basically eliminating the queue line. This had never been done before in a theme park. How would our guests know when to return to ride the attraction? How would this concept be received by our park operations team that, for more than fifty years, had operated these types of attractions in a very traditional manner? These challenges were met head-on by a united team of Imagineers and an *open-minded operations team that had one goal in mind: improving the guest experience.*

*Since the opening of New Fantasyland, the new Dumbo queue has been received with excitement and gratitude by families visiting from around the globe. As with any new attraction, there are always lessons to be learned and challenges to overcome as we work together to craft the perfect guest experience.*

*One important lesson for this team of Imagineers is that when we work together with our partners, we can push the boundaries of what is possible. It's okay to disagree and to be passionate about our ideas and goals even if at times the creative divide seems too great. Ultimately, having differing views and opinions only strengthens the design, and in the end, our guests are the ones who must always benefit. Always lead with the guest experience in mind.*

*As for adding more flying pachyderms to the original menagerie at Dumbo the Flying Elephant, we thought that if watching sixteen elephants fly was amazing, just how great would thirty-two be?*

Outside, the second Dumbo does not simply mirror the first; the vehicles in the new system fly in the opposite direction from the original. Now, as the media reported, the "Double Dumbo Debut" offers guests "twice the Flying Elephant fun!"

And today, I'm on board. After all, Walt's 1941 film is a charmer—so popular that an original Dumbo elephant vehicle from Disneyland was donated to the Smithsonian's National Museum of American History in Washington, D.C., in 2005, during Disneyland's fiftieth anniversary.

# And The Goof goes to . . .

## Astuter Computer Revue in Epcot (1982)

"Some stories move too quickly for 'brick and mortar,'" observes Tom Fitzgerald, now senior vice president of the Imagineering creative group. He's thinking about Astuter Computer Revue, which was one of his first projects as an Imagineer:

> When EPCOT Center was being designed, one of the stories we wanted to tell was about computers. At the time, this conjured up images of huge mainframes and fears of HAL 9000 from the film 2001: A Space Odyssey. So, we decided we'd show how computers helped make the magic at Walt Disney World, and thereby present them in a user-friendly light. We even hired Bob and Dick Sherman to write a song called "My Friend the Computer," to make sure everyone would get the message.
>
> The show would feature a balcony-level view onto the actual control center for Epcot's show systems. Projection screens and special effects magic would allow the show to play for guests without interrupting the work of the technicians within the real-world control space. It was a clever combination of fiction and fantasy—or so we thought.
>
> Then, just as we were putting the finishing touches

*on the show, and getting ready for Epcot's debut, something happened that changed everything. The personal computer took off. Suddenly, everyone wanted one. And our show? Well, it was obsolete before it even opened! Though we did a quick revamp shortly thereafter, we couldn't keep up with the computer story—it was changing, and changing the world, far too quickly for "brick and mortar"!*

In this instance, our guests' shoes moved too quickly and left Astuter Computer at the starting line.

CE OF TREATMENT, PROVIDE A TON OF TREAT
TOP LEARNING • I TELL ONE STORY
UAL MAGNET) • COLLABOR
• I KNOW YOUR
IN IDENTIT

# COMMANDMENT #3

# ORGANIZE THE FLOW
# OF PEOPLE AND IDEAS

The important point here is that great stories, and great experiences, have a logic and sequence that pays off for your guests, customers, or readers for the time and effort they have put in—whether it's reading a story to their kids, walking through a museum exhibit, or plunging into an adventure with marauding pirates.

There are a few exceptions—a mirror maze or a fun house in an old-time amusement park—experiences that intentionally have no clear logic or sequence. But great guest adventures, the stories we want to hear or see or take part in over and over again, are organized in a way that dots all the i's and crosses all the t's. They are clear and understandable. We can explain them to our children—and to ourselves. We know what *they* are, and where *we* are.

No one understood the notion of organizing the flow of people and ideas as well as John Hench. In a 1978 interview with *New West* magazine, John shared his insights:

> If you're at a state fair or something, everything clamors for your attention, so you look and you look and you try to make sense out of things, you try to decide and you constantly make a lot of judgments. But here, when we come to a point in the park that we know is a decision point, we put two choices. We try not to give them seven or eight so that they have to decide in a qualitative way which is the best of those. You just give them two. . . .We unfold these things so that they're normal.

# And the Mousecar Goes to . . .

### Indiana Jones and the Temple of the Forbidden Eye, Disneyland Park, Anaheim

Yes, the experience is one of the best Disney park adventures—so much so that it's also featured at Tokyo DisneySea (as Temple of the Crystal Skull in the Lost River Delta area), and the ride vehicle was used to create Dinosaur! at the Animal Kingdom in Walt Disney World. But it's the amazing half-mile queue in Adventureland at Disneyland that sets a standard unique even for a Disney park.

The Indy queue begins outside, alongside the Jungle Cruise, an appropriate mood-setting pathway of lush trees and vines and jungle sounds. The fifty-thousand-square-foot show building housing the Temple of Doom is your destination—and a key part of the queue experience. Inside, the Spike Room (watch out for those spears!), the Rotunda Calendar (are those large stones moving?), and the show introduction (presented as an old newsreel about the discovery of the tomb) set the stage for the adventure to come.

The ride system is referred to by Disney operators as EMV—Enhanced Motion Vehicle—basically a simulator on wheels with vehicles resembling military troop transports. They pitch and roll and ride up and down, with each carrying twelve passengers through the Chamber of Destiny and the Hall of Promise and past the giant stone carving of Mara's face—flashing fire and light as the vehicle crosses a rickety wooden bridge, under a swaying rope bridge. The ending, where Indiana Jones helps riders escape a giant boulder threatening to crush the vehicle, is a thrill few park attractions have ever matched.

But it's that queue experience that sets the standard for organizing the flow of people and ideas. By the time you reach and board your vehicle, you are thoroughly immersed in the Indiana Jones mystique that George Lucas and Steven Spielberg created in four blockbuster motion pictures. The music, based on the John Williams score from the films, accompanies and enhances the immersive experience.

# And The Goof goes to . . .

## Disney's Animal Kingdom at Walt Disney World

Jack Lindquist, Disneyland's first marketing manager and later its first president, loves to recall the early days of Walt Disney's first Magic Kingdom: "We didn't know *anything*, so we were willing to try *everything*!"

By 1998, however, Disney had acquired an amazing body of knowledge about guests visiting our then nine parks around the world. We could anticipate almost every issue before a new park or attraction opened to the public. Yet when our tenth park, the fourth at Walt Disney World, opened on Earth Day in 1998, we realized we had made the most basic of mistakes. The result: confusion for our early guests.

Here's how the creative leader of the design team, Joe Rohde, explains The Goof:

> *When we designed Animal Kingdom we were working to a high concept based on* adventure. *We wanted the park to feel adventurous. One of our techniques was to obscure the destination at the end of a pathway so that you'd have to walk forward to reveal the destination. A mini-adventure. Often we would curve the pathway just enough so that you couldn't see the other end, but just barely. None of this worked. People just wouldn't walk in a*

*direction where they couldn't see the destination.*

*It wasn't everyone, but from an industrial engineering point of view, it was enough to clog the pathways as crowds backed up behind people who were confused. They needed more reassurance that the pathway led somewhere. So we widened pathways just enough so you could see through, and straightened out those that were too twisty, and people began to move.*

*People are people. They aren't always going to cooperate with your highfalutin concept!*

Disney's Animal Kingdom has become one of the most popular parks in the world, attracting over ten million guests yearly. Once the pathway views were clear to Harambe village, DinoLand, the Festival of the Lion King live show, Kali River Rapids, Maharajah Jungle Trek, the Kilimanjaro Safaris (an adventurous ride across a savanna populated by several hundred African animals, including giraffes, elephants, lions, hippos, cheetahs, and crocodiles), Expedition Everest, and the park's visual and spiritual icon—the 145-foot-tall Tree of Life—Animal Kingdom took its place among the elite Disney park experiences.

Walt Disney World guests can also extend their animal adventure experience by staying nearby at Disney's Animal Kingdom Lodge, a 1,300-room resort where the animals graze in view of guest rooms—creating the feeling that you are enjoying an overnight stay on the edge of the African savanna.

"Our stories aren't just about animals," Joe Rohde points out. "They're about us . . . about our relationship to animals, about what they mean to us, and about what we can mean to them, both good and bad. Even the world we are creating now at Disney's Animal Kingdom, Avatar, with its imaginary animals, is still a metaphor for our real world, the creatures in it, and how we relate to them."

Organizing the sequence and flow of your ideas is not just an idea for theme park storytelling. It's a way of making your presentations more (and most) effective in any medium.

NCE OF TREATMENT, PROVIDE A TON OF TREAT
STOP LEARNING • I TELL ONE STORY
SUAL MAGNET) • COLLABOR
TY • I KNOW YOUR
TAIN IDENTITY
IENC

# COMMANDMENT #4

# CREATE A WIENIE (VISUAL MAGNET)

No, it's not a Nathan's Famous or a Dodger Dog we're talking about—it's Walt Disney's term for visual targets that lead visitors clearly and logically through an experience. Think of the visual magnets that draw you from a distance to a specific target in a Disney park: the castle dominating the end of Main Street; the rocket ship or spinning jets in Tomorrowland; the imposing Chinese Theatre in Disney's Hollywood Studios; Spaceship Earth at Epcot.

Think about this commandment the next time someone asks you for directions to your home. Is there a church spire, a school building, or a natural feature that you can use as a wienie?

One of the first lessons we all learned from the great Disney design chefs was how to cook up a Disney wienie.

The menu includes icons that have become nearly as well known as the Eiffel Tower in Paris, Big Ben in London, or the Unisphere—built as the symbol of the 1964–65 New York World's Fair and still welcoming visitors to Flushing Meadows in the borough of Queens.

In fact, one of Walt Disney's favorite wienies was actually created for that New York World's Fair: the Tower of the Four Winds that called visitors to the inaugural presentation of "it's a small world"—originally a salute to the children of the world for UNICEF, the United Nations Children's Fund.

Years ago, when the first exhibition of treasures from the tomb of Egypt's King Tut first traveled to American museums, the staff at the Los Angeles County Museum of Art asked John Hench to review their layout for the exhibit. According to Hench, they had placed one of the exhibit's true treasures, the boy king's exquisite golden mask, at the very beginning of the exhibition. John told me he immediately saw its location as a showstopper that would impede movement into the exhibition; so he moved it to the very end of the show—making it the visual wienie that helped move the audience into and through the presentation.

# And the Mousecar goes to . . .

### The Fantasyland castles in
### Disney parks around the world

As iconic as the original Disneyland castle is today, as Disneyland celebrates its sixtieth birthday in 2015, it's appropriate to ask why the Imagineers did not simply replicate Sleeping Beauty Castle as the symbol of the Disney parks as they were created around the world. In fact, in the five Magic Kingdom–style parks, there are three different castles— and a fourth style now under construction at Shanghai Disneyland. A wienie not only draws the guest toward a destination but can also serve to establish a unifying theme of an attraction or experience.

The Disneyland castle came with these instructions from the boss: "Make it tall enough to be seen from all around the park. It's got to keep people oriented." In other words, it was the wienie. The first sketch was made by Herb Ryman, who said: "I made it to help sell my friends Dick Irvine's and Marvin Davis's idea—to base it on King Ludwig's Bavarian castle."

But Herb actually took exception to copying a famous European landmark. As Imagineer Randy Bright wrote in *Disneyland: Inside Story*, Ryman pointed out that the Bavarian castle faced backward in the Disneyland plan. One day he picked up the top of the scale model of the castle, turned it completely around, and set it back down with the turrets facing down Main Street. With the model positioned that way, Walt Disney unexpectedly walked into the Model Shop and took an instant liking to Ryman's idea. "End of debate," Bright wrote. "Walt liked the model with the blue roof," Harriet Burns recalled, "because he thought it would blend in with the sky, making the castle look taller."

But when it came time to design a castle for the Magic Kingdom at Walt Disney World, King Ludwig's castle just would not do. Disneyland's version was only seventy-seven feet high, adequate when viewed from a maximum distance of about one-fifth of a mile looking down that park's Main Street, U.S.A., from the train station.

In contrast, on the 28,000-acre Walt Disney World site, Cinderella's Castle would need to stand out more prominently and be seen first from nearly one mile away, when guests arrived at the Transportation and Ticket Center. The castle needed to be much taller to be seen. So the Imagineers made its top spire 189 feet above ground level: tall enough to tower over the low, flat Florida landscape—and a few feet shy of requiring a red light to warn aircraft of its presence.

Cinderella's Castle was duplicated for Tokyo Disneyland, which opened in 1983. But when it came time to create a castle for Disneyland Paris in 1992, the Imagineers realized that neither Disneyland's Sleeping Beauty Castle nor Walt Disney World's Cinderella's Castle would do—we couldn't very well build a German castle outside of Paris, and the French would not welcome a copy of one of their own historic châteaus. A new approach was called for, one that fit the requirements particular to Disneyland Paris.

In the book *Dream it! Do It!*, I quoted Fantasyland's show producer Tom Morris as he recounted (for *Disney Twenty-three* magazine) how the Paris concept emerged and the various creative obstacles were addressed:

> We opted for a fanciful castle that would seem
> to come right out of a European fairy tale. Mont
> Saint-Michel's manner of reaching for the sky, while
> coiling up on itself, was an early inspiration. I went
> on a tour of the castles in the Loire region west of
> Paris (inspiration for Cinderella's Castle at Walt Disney
> World). The windows of Chaumont were interesting,

*the tower at d'Azay-le-Rideau impressed me, some
moats were superb, [and] a specific stained glass
window intrigued me. Inspiration was everywhere.*

*Finally, we wanted to incorporate the "square
trees" from Walt's film* Sleeping Beauty *to give it
an Eyvind Earle sort of look. (Earle, the production
designer for* Sleeping Beauty, *had taken inspiration
from the tapestries in the Cluny Museum in Paris.) So
the story had come full circle.*

*The dramatic Château de la Belle au Bois Dormant
(Sleeping Beauty Castle) blends contemporary French
building techniques (concrete and steel) . . . with
local European crafts: plaster-carving, stained glass
window-making, decorative metalwork, patterned
roof tiles, and tapestries (for the interior). Some of
the companies that accomplished the work had been
in operation for over five hundred years, notably the
tapestry and roof-tile makers.*

The newest Disney castles, both in China, have been
approached in dramatically different and very distinct man-
ners. Hong Kong Disneyland, opened in 2005, based its Main
Street entry on the Anaheim park's Main Street. Therefore, it
was a natural choice to replicate the original Sleeping Beauty
Castle as the wienie beckoning visitors to flow down Main
Street to the Central Plaza, where each of the lands radiates
out from this hub.

But the Shanghai team had a vastly different context—a
very blank page where their imaginations, design talents,
and operational needs had to be totally reimagined for a new
world with unprecedented dynamics—and expectations.

Coulter Winn, creative director for the architecture of Shanghai Disneyland's Enchanted Storybook Castle, gave me an overview of the careful thinking that went into this castle's design:

*In 2010 Bob Weis, the creative executive for the Shanghai Disneyland project, asked me to lead the design for the castle for the Shanghai Disneyland Resort, which was just beginning the "blue sky" or early-design phase. Bob organized a design competition among several WDI designers, architects, and consultants to see if someone could come up with a compelling vision for the castle's design.*

*There were a variety of schemes, but the sketch that won the day was done by Doug Rogers, who had just completed work as the production designer for the movie* Tangled *and had designed that film's castle. Doug's sketch looked more like a French château at the base, which was very different than the walled bases typically supporting Disney castles. The team used Doug's sketch as a road map to begin developing the design.*

*The building program was the most complex of any Disney castle, and featured a castle stage show with support functions for cast and performers; scenes from a boat ride with an underground show, boat storage, and maintenance; retail shops; a 250-seat restaurant; a castle walk-through attraction; character meet-and-greet attractions; a character boutique; secret cloister garden (inspired by Mont Saint-Michel but a lot smaller); a main garden overlook; and a VIP* space. Elevators were required to separate cast and guest traffic but had to be placed so performers could magically appear to entertain the guests. A double-helix grand staircase takes guests to and from the castle walk-through show located on the third floor, as well. In comparison, Cinderella's Castle at Walt Disney World has only a smaller restaurant and a character boutique as its guest programs.

While all the functions were being worked out, the massing of the castle had to be carefully investigated. The trick was to make the castle feel unique, but also feel like a member of the Disney castle family, if you will. This was a daunting task, since a vertical appearance was desired. Once the base began to take shape, the next task was to study how the towers were to be placed on the base to give the castle its Disney identity. This was done with the aid of computer design to allow for many quick studies. The Shanghai castle, at 196 feet, is approximately ten feet taller than Cinderella's Castle in Florida, and 120 feet taller than Sleeping Beauty Castle in Disneyland.

As concept design was completed, I felt the castle still had a bit of an identity problem. A visit to Neuschwanstein Castle in Füssen, Germany, in 2011 gave me the clarity I needed. It is the castle you see in all the German travel posters, perched high up on a hill with valleys and mountains beyond. Neuschwanstein is the castle that heavily influenced the design of the original Disneyland castle. The exterior has a very elegant simplicity to it, which impressed me.

As the design further progressed, a large physical model was built to study the way the castle was positioned on the site. The castles I visited on my first castle research trip impressed me with the way they "met the ground." Sometimes they appeared to be built right out of solid rock, with the biggest stones at the bottom, transitioning to smaller ones as you went up higher. I wanted to capture some of that look to give the castle a believability and elegance. Physical models are very informative tools, which cannot be replaced by virtual models. We always use both at Imagineering.

The design of the castle was a challenging and fun project, and I look forward to seeing guests enjoy it!

# And The Goof goes to . . .

## The World Bazaar Center Street at Tokyo Disneyland

I can hear some of the criticism of my choice of The Goof already. How can you possibly denigrate one of the most successful achievements in the history of the Disney parks? Let me explain.

The Tokyo Disneyland team analyzed all the factors related to building a new park in Urayasu, Chiba Prefecture. Weather was a key consideration. Disney had never built or operated a park where winter cold was a factor. To achieve guest comfort—yes, it rains (and rains!) and sometimes even snows during Tokyo's winter months, and heat and humidity are summer mainstays—our team and the Oriental Land Company, owner of Tokyo Disneyland, determined it was vital to cover and enclose the main street with a glass canopy. Given an international flavor, it became the Victorian-style World Bazaar. While the retail shops, food facilities, and guest services are typical of the open Main Streets in the other Disneyland-style parks around the world, two major changes give Tokyo Disneyland a very different look and initial guest experience.

First, it's the only Magic Kingdom–style park that does not have a train station at the entrance and a railroad encircling the whole park. (The train ride became a separate adventure in the Frontier/Westernland area.)

Second, Center Street—taking its name from its location—bisects the World Bazaar and as a result allows guests to choose a route into the park without actually drawing them to the Central Plaza.

What ought to have been perhaps the best wienie in any Disney park, with the glass canopy structure framing Cinderella's Castle perfectly as you look through the World Bazaar to the center of the park, instead is now diminished by the presence of two escape routes. Turn east on Center Street, walk a few paces, and you are suddenly in Adventureland. Turn west, and ahead of you, at the end of that vista, is Tomorrowland.

It's been this way for more than thirty years, since Tokyo Disneyland opened on April 12, 1983. And I would venture to say that only a handful of the millions and millions of guests visiting Tokyo Disneyland have ever thought twice about the Center Street issue. But that doesn't make it right. It's true, I am a Disney purist when it comes to the importance of guest orientation and the castle's role. "Make it tall enough to be seen from all around the park," Walt told Herb Ryman. "It's got to keep people oriented."

We always learn from our experiences. So for me, Center Street in Tokyo Disneyland has earned The Goof award. Notice, please, that the Imagineers have never repeated that layout in any subsequent park.

NCE OF TREATMENT, PROVIDE A TON OF TREAT
STOP LEARNING • I TELL ONE STORY
ISUAL MAGNET) • COLLABOR
TY • I KNOW YOUR A
TAIN IDENTIT
RIENC

# COMMANDMENT #5

# COMMUNICATE WITH VISUAL LITERACY

Having started my Disney career as a writer in Disneyland's public relations department, I had always thought of reading and writing as the major reference points for literacy. But in one of my first discussions with John Hench, he used the term "visual literacy."

Although few Imagineers were as literate as John, we all understood his point. As designers and storytellers, we make use of nonverbal ways to communicate: color, shape, form, texture.

Hench expanded on his explanation in his excellent book *Designing Disney—Imagineering and the Art of the Show*, published by Disney Editions in 2004:

*We pay close attention to color relationships and how they help us to tell our stories. Nothing in a theme park is seen in isolation. . . . We visualize the buildings and their facades next to one another, and also in the context of the surrounding pavement, the landscape, the sky with its changing weather, as well as the props and decorative furnishings that might be adjacent to these structures. . . . Color assists guests in making decisions because it establishes the identity of each attraction in the park.*

To be an effective communicator, make sure you take advantage of all the nonverbal tools you have at your command.

# And the Mousecar goes to . . .

## The World Showcase in Epcot, Walt Disney World

I was doubly blessed on the day in the late 1970s when Disney Legend Fred Joerger came to my office with a suggestion: "What would you think if we could get Harper Goff to come work on the Epcot project?"

My first blessing had been Fred Joerger himself. The great model maker, along with Harriet Burns and Wathel Rogers, had defined dimensional design at Imagineering. But early in 1979, after twenty-five years, Fred retired. Before the year

was out, I had played on my friendship with Fred—and my creative responsibilities for the Epcot project—to convince him to unretire and become the field art director of the new park.

Wouldn't you do everything possible to get the person on your team who had been responsible for assuring that Pirates of the Caribbean, the Submarine Voyage, and other signature attractions achieved the look that Imagineering's art directors had designed?

My second blessing was that Fred Joerger's friend Harper Goff was looking for a new project to jump into. Here was the opportunity for another great Disney Legend to come full circle in his career. Harper had drawn some of the early concepts for Disneyland's Main Street, U.S.A.—some say they were reminiscent of Harper's birthplace in Fort Collins, Colorado—and then conceived the menacing exterior and plush Victorian interior for the *Nautilus* submarine in Walt's *20,000 Leagues Under the Sea*.

What would I think if we could get Harper Goff to work on Epcot? Come on, Fred—be serious!

*Communicate with visual literacy.* It's hard to think of

an illustration among the nearly two hundred thousand in Imagineering's vault—all the drawings by Herb Ryman, John Hench, Marc Davis, Claude Coats, Sam McKim, Harper Goff, etc.—that does this better than Goff's painting illustrating the relationships of the countries of the World Showcase. Harper's illustrations, and others by Dorothea Redmond and Collin Campbell, often highlighted instantly recognizable architectural features. They speak volumes about the importance of communicating to our guests with visual literacy.

My former partner in leading the Imagineers, Mickey Steinberg, recently wrote to me about the suspension of disbelief guests experience in projects the Imagineers design. "No one can create spaces that allow you to suspend disbelief better than the Imagineers," Mickey wrote. "For a short time, children really believe they are in a magic land even though they know they are in Florida. For a short while, my sister-in-law believed she was in Paris when she really knew she was in Florida."

Thank you, Harper—for this concept and the design

concepts for the pavilions of Japan, Italy, Germany, Morocco, and the United Kingdom.

And—thank you, Fred Joerger!

# And The Goof goes to . . .

## The Haunted Mansion in Disneyland

I'm getting into trouble on this one . . . but I have to be honest about it. Part of my reluctance in critiquing Walt Disney himself is that Walt really liked something I wrote that reinforced *his concept*, and now I am about to criticize it.

On the facing page is the sign copy that appeared outside Disneyland's Haunted Mansion beginning in 1965—four years before the attraction opened in 1969.

Remembering that we are dealing with Mickey's Commandment # 5—"Communicate with Visual Literacy"— here's the issue: this mansion does not look haunted from the outside. In fact, the exterior of the building was arguably designed and built before a show had been developed for the inside. And that is *not* the way good storytelling is accomplished.

I don't think Walt would have approached the concept this way if not for the fact that Imagineering, at the time the exterior was built, was almost totally focused on creating the four Disney shows for the 1964–65 New York World's Fair. This was in 1963, long before there were grim grinning ghosts, Doom Buggies to carry you through the attraction, and Madame Leota waiting to tell your fortune.

Walt stated Disney would maintain a pristine mansion "on the outside . . . and the ghosts will practice their post-lifetime skills on the inside." When he was interviewed in the United Kingdom in the early 1960s and asked what he was doing there, he responded, "Gathering ghosts who don't want to retire for my Haunted Mansion." So it really didn't matter what the exterior of that building conveyed. You knew *the inside* would be very special.

And what fun it was for me to be able to communicate that in "verbal literacy" on that exterior sign.

CE OF TREATMENT, PROVIDE A TON OF TREAT
STOP LEARNING • TELL ONE STORY
SUAL MAGNET) • COLLABOR
• I KNOW YOUR A
AIN IDENTIT
ENG

# COMMANDMENT #6

# AVOID OVERLOAD— CREATE TURN-ONS

Your first task on any new project is to learn as much as you can about the subject of your story or assignment. Your second task is to become a great editor. Resist the temptation to overload your audience with everything you have learned, with *too much* information and *too many* objects.

When the Imagineers were designing Epcot at Walt Disney World, I frequently told our staff we were creating *turn-ons* about the subject of each major pavilion: energy, transportation, food, health, communications, space.

First they needed to become experts on their assigned subjects. Then they needed to synthesize what they had learned for our attractions, shows, and exhibits. One example: Peggie Fariss, working with outside authorities on the history of communications for Spaceship Earth, completed her assignment with a bibliography of information sources that filled nineteen typewritten pages. She could tell us about the language of the Egyptian pharaohs and explain ancient Greek drama—all as background for our designers creating the eight-minute ride through Spaceship Earth. What the designers communicated visually, and through the narration heard in the traveling vehicles, had to be reduced from Peggie's multiple pages to a few seconds about each historical event we depicted.

Remember: You are not a contestant on television's *Jeopardy*. In just a few statements in sight and sound, make the audience excited about the subject—make them want to know more!

# And the Mousecar goes to . . .

## Peter Pan's Flight, Fantasyland, Disneyland

Overload in an entertainment experience can sometimes be too much of a good thing. In contrast, sometimes an idea or experience in its most simple and direct form will win the day.

I am in awe of the early, original Imagineers who became Walt's design and production teams at WED Enterprises. Most of them came to Disney park storytelling and design after spending years as leaders in Disney Studios film and television productions, especially the animation world of background painters, color stylists, and character artists.

Mr. Toad and Timothy Mouse and Wendy Darling and Peter Pan were not just household names. Some of the early Imagineers had lived with these stars for weeks and months as they brought their characters to life on the screen.

But living with Tink and Pan and Captain Hook on your drawing board for months is one thing. Translating a seventy-six-minute animated film into a two- to three-minute experience is quite another. It may seem easy to avoid overload when you have less than three minutes to tell your story. But imagine for a moment that you are sitting down with Disney Legends Ken Anderson, Claude Coats, Bill Martin, and Yale Gracey at their drawing boards with an assignment from Walt: Give our guests the thrill of flying in a suspended pirate galleon over moonlit London. Caution:

1. There is no such ride system in existence.
2. You cannot use halogen lightbulbs, touch screen control consoles, 3-D modeling, computer programming, LED lights, etc., *because none of them were available in 1955.*

While there have been refinements made for Peter Pan's Flight through the years—including a major refreshment in 2015—the most popular "dark ride" ever created is still Peter Pan's Flight in a pirate galleon suspended by an overhead cable system. Or perhaps I should say it's *your flight* with Peter Pan. And sixty years later, it's still the simple adventure that has created turn-ons and avoided overload since Disneyland Day One on July 17, 1955.

As author Ray Bradbury wrote, "Disney makes many mistakes; what artist doesn't? But when he flies, he really flies. I shall be indebted to him for a lifetime for his ability to let me fly over midnight London looking down on that fabulous city, in his Peter Pan ride."

# And The Goof goes to . . .

## "America, " produced by Disney Legend Bob Jani at Radio City Music Hall

Anyone privileged to know Robert F. Jani recognizes that as vice president of entertainment for Disney, or as the producer who revitalized Radio City Music Hall in New York City in the 1970s, and even as an event-industry producer (notably the U.S. Bicentennial Celebration in 1976 in New York Harbor), he was among a handful of giants in his field. Just say "Electrical Parade" to any Disney park fan and you know where its producer, Bob Jani, belongs in the rankings of major creative forces.

Jani's foundation in show business was at Disney, but one show Bob produced and presented in the 1970s at Radio City Music Hall—after he had left Disney and created Robert F. Jani Productions—has served as a reminder that you can fall in love with your medium and its potential and overload your audience to such an extent that you actually create turn-*offs*.

I recall turning to my wife, Leah, as we watched and listened to the first few salutes to the fifty American states. "Do you realize," I said quietly, "that we're only at number four? He's going to present an encyclopedia of all fifty states in order, and there are forty-six more. It's going to be a long evening!"

Bob loved America. So many of his iconic productions inside and outside Disney were patriotic tours de force. But once I realized what we were in for that day at Radio City Music Hall, those last forty-six states provided a lesson for me: never overload your audience with your own turn-ons. The audience may be on the same page when you begin, but everyone does not read at the same pace. And if you are not careful, you may not even be reading from the same book.

WEAR YOUR GUESTS SHOES • PASSION • 3 ORGANIZ
TY • 9 FOR EVERY OUNCE OF TREATMENT, PR
ION—NEVER STOP LEARNING • 7 TELL
IAL MAGNET) • COLLABOR
KNOW YOUR AUDIE
TAKE A CH

# COMMANDMENT #7

# TELL ONE STORY AT A TIME

Good stories are clear, logical, and consistent. Stick to the story line.

In the 1930s, the Disney Studios invented the use of storyboards—four-foot-by-eight-foot panels with a surface that sketches and other ideas could be pinned to. They are now used throughout the entertainment industry and in other fields as well. Storyboards are a must in our work, as a way to develop our story sequences.

The objective is to create a story line that holds together from the first sketch to the last. We try to find the holes in the story, correct them, build the action in a scene where necessary, and ultimately to create a clear story line that we can review with any discipline so that everyone who will be involved in building it understands the project's centerpiece: the story.

A storyboard review can help reveal a key point or a weak character that can be reworked without tossing out all the good material the creators have developed. When our team reviewed the concept for Mickey's PhilharMagic with then Disney CEO Michael Eisner, he liked everything but the key character. "Tinker Bell is too *sweet*," he said. "We need some *conflict*. Why don't you try Donald Duck?" It was an inspired suggestion, injecting just the right tone into the show; after all, doesn't Donald always try to upstage Mickey Mouse, resulting in pratfalls and embarrassment?

Now our story was clear and logical. We all stuck to the new story line, and Mickey's PhilharMagic remains a big hit, from Florida's Magic Kingdom to Hong Kong.

And you don't need a four-foot-by-eight-foot panel to create a series of sketches or ideas that illustrate a story. Try thumbnail sketches—very rough drawings as small as two inches by two inches that you can quickly create, easily review, and use to communicate the story idea simply and effectively.

# And the Mousecar goes to . . .

## The Carousel of Progress

- New York World's Fair 1964–65
- Disneyland 1967–1972
- Magic Kingdom, Walt Disney World 1975–Present

The story of how technology changed our world is one that Walt Disney wanted to tell from the earliest days at Disneyland. In fact, one of my first assignments in 1957 was to create a sales booklet outlining the story Walt intended to tell. The booklet described a project called Edison Square that was originally planned as a new side street branching off Main Street, U.S.A. in Disneyland.

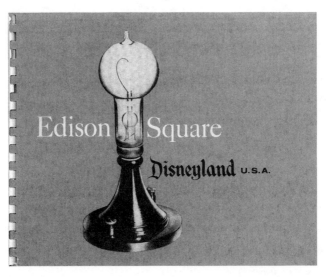

Walt was influenced in his early thinking about Edison Square by his visits to Henry Ford's Greenfield Village in Dearborn, Michigan. Over the years, Ford had acquired some of the iconic birthplaces of American ingenuity, including Thomas Edison's original laboratory, relocated—lock, stock, and lightbulb—from Menlo Park, New Jersey. Walt Disney's love of American history, and his respect for the men and women whose genius paved the way to our nation's leadership in so many fields, led him to initiate new ventures in storytelling about their accomplishments.

Notwithstanding the impressive illustrations by Sam

McKim, John Hench, Herb Ryman, and Paul Hartley, and the organization by WED's president Bill Cottrell, Edison Square never made it beyond the concept stage. So when General Electric came calling to seek Walt Disney's help in creating their pavilion for the 1964–65 New York World's Fair, Edison Square suddenly had a new life.

The first question was how to handle the enormous number of people who would be coming to the fair (which ultimately attracted fifty million visitors in its two seasons). In early concept, Edison Square in Disneyland was designed as a walk-through attraction, where guests would use their own foot power to move from stage set to stage set as the sequenced story of progress through electricity unfolded.

Even in the very best situations, processing as many as a thousand people per hour is an accomplishment—but totally inadequate for a world's fair venue.

Walt also knew that GE wanted to simplify the story of electricity's impact—at least in the major attraction that would draw guests to their pavilion. So two key objectives were established:

- First, the show had to be able to handle at least 2,500 people per hour.
- Second, whatever else would be presented in the GE pavilion, Walt's featured show should be about the impact of electrical products *in the home*.

The first objective was met by Roger Broggie and the Disney Studio machine shop. The Carousel of Progress has a theoretical capacity of 3,600 people per hour. From a show standpoint, Walt and the WED designers had transposed the Edison Square walk-through story into a four-act "play" with a prologue and epilogue. The unique concept was that the show scenes were located *at the center of the theater*—and the audience, traveling in six moving auditoriums, *rode around the central stages*. Imagine a doughnut: your seats are located in the part you would eat. The empty center of the doughnut is filled with all the show sets, Audio-Animatronics figures, lighting, and the technology that runs the production.

"Welcome to the Carousel of Progress," the narrator, originally western film star Rex Allen, intones. "Now, most carousels just go round and round without getting anywhere—but on this one, at every turn, we'll be making progress."

It's the ideal format for telling one story at a time—and for that story to go on and on and on—still entertaining audiences half a century after its debut.

Today the Carousel of Progress is the longest continuously presented theater show in the world. And even now, there's no reason to change the first three acts—representing the 1890s, 1920s, and 1940s. It's still presenting the same history today that it was at its first New York World's Fair appearance in 1964. What has changed is the final act, representing the present day, new products for the home, and the changing roles of women, youth, and grandparents. The Carousel show has attempted to represent many of those changes.

There's no question that the song Dick and Bob Sherman wrote especially for the Carousel of Progress is a key part of its enduring legacy, as it continues to engage audiences at Walt Disney World's Magic Kingdom:

**There's a Great Big Beautiful Tomorrow**
**Richard M. and Robert B. Sherman**

*There's a Great Big Beautiful Tomorrow*
*Shining at the end of every day*
*There's a Great Big Beautiful Tomorrow*
*And tomorrow's just a dream away*

*Man has a dream*
*And that's the start*
*He follows his dream with mind and heart*
*And when it becomes a reality*
*It's a dream come true for you and me*

*So There's a Great Big Beautiful Tomorrow*
*Shining at the end of every day*
*There's a Great Big Beautiful Tomorrow*
*Just a dream away*

These lyrics continue to inspire our hopes and dreams for the future—and they help tell the singular story presented in the Carousel of Progress.

# And The Goof goes to . . .

## Exxon in Epcot and the challenges of corporate sponsorships

I spent many years of my career working with the corporate sponsors of Disney park shows, most notably for Epcot, and before that for the pavilions Walt created for the 1964–65 New York World's Fair. Those corporate sponsors (Disney calls them participants), with their financial support, often determine whether an attraction, show, or pavilion is built at all.

In my experience, the most challenging participant we ever worked with was Exxon, the original sponsor of Epcot's Universe of Energy pavilion (now Ellen's Energy Adventure). Small wonder that they are extremely deserving of The Goof award for ignoring this commandment.

The challenge for the Imagineers and Disney park operators is that our guests come to the Disney parks to be entertained. They expect all the attractions, live entertainment, parades, and character shows to be Disney created (as they are) and have the Disney seal of approval. That's why all signage for sponsored attractions states the name of the show or attraction first, followed by a "Presented by" and the name of the participant. It's meant to be very literal: they are *presenting* a Disney show and are proud of it.

I received my baptism in working with major corporations at the 1964–65 New York World's Fair. To understand the objectives of the Ford Motor Company, for example, John

Hench and I spent weeks visiting Ford facilities in Dearborn and Romeo, Michigan; Philadelphia; and Newport Beach and Palo Alto, California. I give Ford credit for understanding that telling one story at a time could add up to a complete picture of the company in the early 1960s. The result was an integrated, sequential presentation that depicted Ford as an international company with a rich history, working to create better products for tomorrow. One of those better products was a highlight of the fair's opening day: the introduction of a new Ford model, the Mustang. (The culmination of guests' visits to the pavilion was the Disney Magic Skyway ride, where they rode in full-size Ford convertibles—including the new Mustang—through the eight-minute show.)

So that's my gold standard for working positively and successfully with a corporation. At the other extreme—and therefore my choice for The Goof award—was Exxon. They wanted so much information included in the show, much of it their marketing hyperbole, that there was no way we could tell a balanced story if we accepted everything Exxon wanted to say.

The most frustrated Imagineer was Randy Bright, my associate in charge of development of Epcot scripts and shows. Randy elected to write this script himself and quickly discovered that our sponsor seemed to be ignoring three of our commandments: Avoid Overload, Know Your Audience, and especially Tell One Story at a Time. Randy set a record for total number of scripts written before we agreed with Exxon on the one to be given the green light for production: it was the *thirty-ninth* version Randy had written.

There are many examples of companies that have understood the role and responsibility of each party in developing sponsored shows and pavilions in Disney parks around the world. I personally remember fondly the opportunity to work with great companies and their CEOs: William Beers of Kraft, Harry Gray of United Technologies, Roger Smith of General Motors. The people they assigned to work with Imagineering played their roles with an understanding of what the partnership with Disney entailed. Some at Exxon did, too. I had great relationships with two executives, Jack Clarke and Elliot Cattarulla, that have continued for many years. But some of our Exxon contacts forgot the rules, and to show for it today (now that their sponsorship of the pavilion has ended), they have The Goof award they so well deserved.

SSION • 3 ORGANIZE THE FLOW OF PEOPLE AND THE
CE OF TREATMENT, PROVIDE A TON OF TREAT
STOP LEARNING • TELL ONE STORY
SUAL MAGNET) • COLLABOR
D) • I KNOW YOUR
AIN IDENTITY
ENG

# COMMANDMENT #8

# AVOID CONTRADICTIONS— MAINTAIN IDENTITY

Walk down almost any modern main street in any city and you will know the importance of this commandment: everything seems to shout at you for attention—the buildings, the signs, the colors, the sounds. They say: "Look at me!" "Come this way!" "Buy my product!"

Contrast that to the Main Street in any of the Magic Kingdoms. City Hall almost appears to be in friendly conversation with the Opera House or the Theater across the Town Square. No color in any building shouts at you louder than any of its neighbors. All the graphics seem to be equal in stature. As a visitor, you know where you are, and every detail reinforces the time period and the experience. Even though you have never been there, somehow you and your family are at home here. You know, as the dedication plaque in the Town Square states, you are welcome in "this happy place."

We can't all turn the clock back to 1890, but we can work hard to maintain the identity of our setting or story. Eliminating the things that contradict what we are seeing and saying makes our guests feel at home, whether we are in yesterday, today, or tomorrow.

# And the Mousecar goes to . . .

## Shanghai Disneyland for its cultural sensitivity and advance planning

The past, as rich and full of teachings and achievements as it may be, is still a prologue to Disney's future projects, none of which is as significant and full of potential as the Shanghai Disneyland Resort.

Imagineering's senior creative executive leading the Shanghai project teams is Bob Weis. I asked Bob, "How do you plan to 'maintain identity' with Disney traditions when the cultural differences are so pronounced on the Chinese mainland?" His response:

*One thing we learned from you is know your audience. In the case of China, that initially meant reaching out and trying to get to know a culture that we as Americans really knew nothing about. So in the early stages we spent a lot of time traveling and* going to as many good and bad tourism spots, hotels, museums, other public venues as we could.

We also did just plain home visits, met families, visited schools to talk to teachers and students, etc. Then we started to put together really rough ideas of a park menu—mostly drawn from photos of Walt Disney World and Disneyland, and did focus groups all over—and all ages, grandparents, parents, young adults, college students, kids. We let them tear apart our ideas and we listened carefully. We did not design by committee, but we did listen to what seemed to work and what needed too much explanation.

Western and Frontier, for instance, just didn't play for anybody. Neither did trains. Things like that. Pirates was critiqued as too passive and boring. We contacted travel companies and got student groups visiting the United States and Disneyland to meet with us and talk about their experiences.

We also used our partners for their insights into their own families and communities and had them work with us on critiquing everything from the castle to dining to Pirates. If they didn't get it, we knew we had work to do.

The big thing we did was I wanted Chinese on our team, not just as advisers. I wanted Chinese Imagineers and we didn't have any. So we built them, brought in mainland Chinese artists, writers, architects, and we learned China from them, and they learned Disney from us. They remain some of our most valuable team members, and many are going *to be just great Imagineers, in China or elsewhere.*

*The overwhelming majority of our team in Shanghai is also Chinese. They are shaping menus, retail products, operating styles, colors, everything to do with how the park will look and feel. Our scripts are being written by native Mandarin speakers—written, not translated. The show vendors are all working in China, so we're working directly with Chinese artists, sculptors, painters, and exchanging perceptions and techniques.*

*Our executive chefs are Shanghainese. We've used one of China's most lauded typography artists to do themed Chinese on our marquees. Marquees still include themed English, but we have been more expressive with the Chinese, and it's yielded a very unique, exciting cultural blend.*

*Our goal is still Disney, yet it will be distinctly Chinese, as it's been developed and had many contributions from our Chinese cast and Imagineers. It will not feel like Tokyo, or Hong Kong, or Paris; it will have its own feeling. We even have, for the first time ever, bilingual name tags.*

The verdict, of course, will be rendered only when Shanghai Disneyland is open to the expected millions of Chinese and other visitors from across Asia. But the advance planning and inclusive design approach by Bob Weis and the Imagineers is already setting a new planning standard. As Bob said, "Our goal is still Disney"—we'll maintain our identity—but "it will be distinctly Chinese."

# And The Goof goes to . . .

## Le Visionarium: Un Voyage à Travers le Temps, Euro Disneyland at opening 1992 (replaced by Buzz Lightyear Laser Blast in 2006)

At one of the first meetings we had with the Oriental Land Company (OLC) about Tokyo Disneyland in the late 1970s (for the resort that opened in April 1983), the OLC team cautioned us about doing a project in Japan: "Don't 'Japanize' us!" What did this mean?

Quick studies that we are, we deciphered the message: the Japanese are a relatively small, homogeneous population—about one-hundred million in the entire nation. Don't try to tell *them* about *them*: They came to us for Disney and America.

It's too bad our French partners were not attending those meetings. In contrast, discussions with the French government resulted in an agreement to create a special show for Euro Disneyland (now Disneyland Paris). They felt strongly that the people coming to the park would expect to see an attraction showcasing French history and culture. *"Vive la France!"* someone remarked.

The show, called The Timekeeper or Le Visionarium: Un Voyage à Travers le Temps, had all the ingredients for success. It opened in the park's most elaborate and distinctive area, Discoveryland, a Jules Verne–inspired version of the Tomorrowlands in other Disney parks. The concept and design of Discoveryland paid homage to the European visionaries of the past, and how they might have envisioned the future. Space Mountain, with its cannon-blast vehicle launch, a visit to the *Nautilus* submarine, and the elegant flying Orbitron also emphasized the visionary theme.

Yet by 2006, Le Visionarium had been replaced by Buzz Lightyear Laser Blast—the Paris version of Disneyland's Buzz Lightyear Space Rangers Spin and Tokyo Disneyland's Buzz Lightyear Astro Blasters.

What went wrong? One of the challenges in Paris is the variety of European cultures Disneyland Paris attracts. Unlike the homogeneous population in Japan, Disneyland Paris's audience is a European stew. While the majority of visitors are French, large numbers of guests also come from the United Kingdom, Spain, Germany, Italy, and northern and eastern Europe. Despite the European Union, there is no European identity.

Mickey Steinberg, who left Disney in 1994 after five years as my partner at Imagineering, running the administrative, finance, and project management side of our business, was one of the people most responsible for the opening success of Disneyland Paris. Before and after his time at Disney, Mickey had extensive international experience leading the engineering and architectural project development work for Atlanta architect John Portman's projects in the United States, as well as in China and Europe. With his background, Steinberg knew the conditions and warned us about dealing with other cultures and provided thoughtful caution:

*You should discuss the amount of research and use of judgment that the designer must do to determine the extent that his/her design concept fits the culture and does not offend the sensibilities of the audience. This is especially true when you are dealing with characters and brands such as Disney. You have to determine if they are understood, if they offend, if they are loved, etc.*

*Then you have to determine if you can use English and on and on. If you misjudge it, then you have committed an error that will guarantee failure. You have to truly understand an audience that is foreign to you in the true sense of the word. That is an unforgiving and, therefore, very difficult task.*

"In Japan," says Imagineering creative executive Daniel Jue, "for every attraction we try to find some localization identity. That's not simply translating but rather adapting the show content to maximize our guests' understanding and enjoyment of the show." And with that identity, the chances of avoiding contradictions that mislead or even offend are greatly enhanced.

"Do your homework," says creative leader and show writer Kevin Rafferty. "Good storytelling is good storytelling. But—never assume." In the new Ratatouille attraction in Paris, Kevin points out, a character says a line in French while another character repeats the same thought in English. Character one (in French): "Let's go this way!" Character two (in English): "Okay, we're going this way!"

In Le Visionarium, we forgot that what we presented was not universally understood—especially with the dynamic and diversified cultures of Europe. No universal understanding or identity was established—probably because there was none to be created. In these circumstances, avoiding contradictions may not have been possible, making it improbable that the show could succeed.

CE OF TREATMENT, PROVIDE A TON OF TREAT
STOP LEARNING · I TELL ONE STORY
SUAL MAGNET) · COLLABOR
· I KNOW YOUR A
AIN IDENTIT
ENO

# COMMANDMENT #9

# FOR EVERY OUNCE OF TREATMENT, PROVIDE A TON OF TREAT

Remember the song lyrics Julie Andrews sang in *Mary Poppins*: "A spoonful of sugar helps the medicine go down." Bob and Dick Sherman had it exactly right for anyone in the fun business. As Walt Disney told us, we can educate—but in a Disney park, we don't label it; we let you *discover*, and hopefully *learn*, surrounded by adventures, music, songs, and visual treats. First and foremost we do everything we can to *make it fun*.

Walt truly established that learning can be fun with attractions like Rocket to the Moon when Disneyland opened in 1955. Calling upon space pioneers, including the scientist Wernher von Braun, to work with his artists and writers,

Walt created the realistic experience of traveling in space and landing on the moon—fourteen years before it actually happened.

Later he created Great Moments with Mr. Lincoln for the 1964–65 New York World's Fair; it opened a year later in Disneyland's Opera House. And when Walt Disney World opened in 1971, the Imagineers fulfilled Walt Disney's complete vision for a Hall of Presidents, where the actual words of our national leaders inspire us about the past, and the future, of our great nation.

I believe that the very fact we've placed these kinds of shows in Disney parks tells our guests that these attractions are as much a part of a Disney family fun experience as Pirates of the Caribbean or the Haunted Mansion. Walt made educating visitors an integral part of the Disney park experience—without ever using that word. Who can ever forget the message of "it's a small world," where the children of many nations tell us in song that "there is just one moon and one golden sun, and a smile means friendship to everyone"?

The acceptance by Disney park guests of these shows as part of the fun fabric of their visit established the background for the development of Epcot at Walt Disney World. As students ourselves who research every assignment in depth, the Imagineers knew there were wonderful stories to tell about the world's energy challenges, new discoveries in the oceans' depths, and exciting ways to grow food for a hungry planet. All we had to do was follow the advice of Mary Poppins: "A spoonful of sugar helps the medicine go down, in a most delightful way!"

# And the Mousecar goes to . . .

**"it's a small world," originally created for the 1964–65 New York World's Fair, now in Disneyland Park, the Magic Kingdom, Tokyo Disneyland, Disneyland Paris, and Hong Kong Disneyland**

**It's a Small World**
**Richard M. and Robert B. Sherman**

*It's a world of laughter, a world of tears*
*It's a world of hopes and a world of fears*
*There's so much that we share*
*That it's time we're aware*
*It's a Small World after all.*

*There is just one moon and one golden sun*
*And a smile means friendship to ev'ryone*
*Though the mountains divide*
*And the oceans are wide*
*It's a Small World after all.*

It seemed as though almost without exception that wherever I spoke to audiences after the publication of *Dream It! Do It!*, someone would ask this question: "What is your favorite Disney park attraction?" There were reasons from time to time that I wanted to give other answers—Pirates of the Caribbean or Space Mountain.

But in the end I always tell my audiences, "There is just one moon and one golden sun, and a smile means friendship to everyone." What greater family fun lesson could we present to the millions of guests each year who ride the canal boats along the waterways that connect the children of the world? There are teachable moments everywhere in the joy of children attired in their native finery, singing and dancing and reminding us that "there's so much that we share that it's time we're aware it's a small world after all."

One of the great privileges of my career, before I became the creative leader of the Imagineers, was writing special (and often personal) material for Walt Disney's signature—essentially ghostwriting for Walt.

Although I had spent most of my career at Imagineering, including thirty years as the leader of the creative storytellers and designers, I never escaped my roots as a writer. After all, I was hired in June of 1955, one month before Disneyland opened, to create *The Disneyland News*, to be sold for ten cents on Main Street—it was Disneyland's hometown newspaper. Plus, I had written dozens of presentations to sell new projects to sponsors, media, and the public, and so many introductions to books about the Disney parks that I lost count years ago.

When I reflect on all the communications I wrote over that half century, none compares to the privilege and thrill of writing words that would be read or heard with Walt Disney's name, voice, and signature. I wrote his messages in the 1960s-era company annual reports, introductions for Disneyland's early souvenir guidebooks, presentations that introduced the company (and Walt and Roy Disney) at the November 1965 press conference in Orlando that announced the Walt Disney World project, and the script for the very last time Walt appeared on film. It was late October 1966, and the film—completed after Walt's death—was his introduction to the Florida project and his concept for Epcot: Experimental Prototype Community of Tomorrow.

Writing words to appear in print, or to be recorded for film or television, in Walt Disney's name and persona was the experience of this writer's lifetime. I was in my twenties when I received that first assignment, and just past thirty when I wrote that script for the Epcot film. Walt had made it so easy for me. I still have the seven pages of notes I made from two meetings in Walt's office to discuss the film, and what he wanted to emphasize and communicate.

Learning to use words and phrases that communicated the ideas and plans envisioned by one of the great creative storytellers and entrepreneurs of the twentieth century was truly an education. Early on I discovered a book titled *Words to Live By*, published in the 1940s, containing one- or two-page inspiring messages from leaders in many fields about their experiences and careers. Walt's was called "Take a Chance." It not only embodied his risk-taking philosophy, but it was written in a tone and style that sounded and felt like the Walt Disney I was getting to know. I had found the Walt style I would emulate in scripts, publications, and narrations, like the one Walt recorded for the Magic Skyway ride Imagineering designed for the Ford pavilion at the 1964–65 New York World's Fair.

Which brings me full circle to one of my treasured assignments: creating the *Complete Souvenir Guide and Behind the Scenes Story* about "it's a small world"—sold at the 1964–65 New York World's Fair, where the attraction was first presented. The introduction I wrote for Walt Disney's signature is still one of my favorites, for its simplicity and economy of words—but certainly not economy of meaning:

*"To all who come to this happy place . . .*
*welcome."*
*These words, engraved on its dedication plaque,*
*symbolize the warm and friendly spirit of Disneyland,*
*our Magic Kingdom in Anaheim, California.*
*Now we have created another kind of "magic*
*kingdom," with its world premiere at this New York*
*World's Fair. In theme, and in its festive spirit, we have*
*tried to make this new "land" the happiest of places . . .*
*"a magic kingdom of all the world's children."*
*We call this adventure "It's a Small World." All of*
*us who participated in its creation hope that your ride*
*through our Small World is a memorable experience*
*for you and your family.*
*"To all who come to this happy place . . .*
*welcome."*

**Walt Disney**

If you consider the example Walt set in "it's a small world" to be a lesson or treatment, there's no question that this attraction provides a ton of treat. We are so fortunate that Walt's lesson plan, couched in its finest family fun, still inspires children of all ages fifty years after it first communicated the words Dick and Bob Sherman wrote: "Though the mountains divide, and the oceans are wide, it's a small world after all."

# And The Goof goes to . . .

## Disneyland, for removal of the House of the Future at the entrance to Tomorrowland

Nothing in our visual literacy vocabulary said "Tomorrowland" better than the House of the Future. It was an inspiration even to future Imagineers.

"Little did I know on a visit to Disneyland as a child in 1966 that seeing the House of the Future in Tomorrowland would make such an impact in my life, that it would affect me and inspire me years later to choose architecture as a career," designer Oscar Cobos Jr. of Imagineering's Architectural Design Studio recalled. "This House of the Future awakened in me the possibilities of how the built environment could affect our lives. With my love for art, drawing, physics, and mathematics, architecture was a natural choice where I could practice all those topics I enjoyed and loved."

A relationship of mutual respect and admiration between Walt Disney and the distinguished scientist/chemist Charles Thomas, president and later chairman of Monsanto, resulted in creating three important attractions for the early Tomorrowland in Disneyland: first, at the park's official opening, the Monsanto Hall of Chemistry exhibit; second, the Monsanto House of the Future; and third, Adventure Thru Inner Space—one of the most popular ride-through experiences in the park (especially with teenagers) from its opening in 1967 until it was closed in 1985 to make room for Star Tours.

The all-plastic House of the Future was easily the most futuristic structure in Tomorrowland. It stood on an elevated central pedestal, with four wings cantilevering out from the central core. The design and engineering was a joint effort among Monsanto, the Massachusetts Institute of Technology, and Walt Disney Imagineering. It opened in 1957 and was removed in 1967.

While its purpose was to demonstrate the use of plastics in construction and inside the home—where it looked into the "future" of 1986 and featured ahead-of-their-time products, including the microwave oven, ultrasonic dishwasher, "cold zones" (to replace refrigerators and freezers), and dimmable ceiling lights—the House of the Future had a *Jetsons* look and feel about it.

There are lots of things we don't miss about those early Disneyland days—the original character costumes, borrowed from the Ice Capades show where Disney had licensed the use of Mickey, Minnie, and other characters; the Hollywood-Maxwell Brassiere Co. shop on Main Street (right next door to Grandma's Baby Shop), featuring "intimate apparel, brassieres, and torsolettes" and the "Wonderful Wizard of Bras" exhibit; or the Bathroom of the Future, sponsored by the Crane Company in Tomorrowland. But unlike those "forgotten" features, the House of the Future provided a "ton of treat."

Even today, part of the legacy of the House of the Future is its removal from the park—which in actuality was never totally completed. The removal process added to its legend when crews were unable to demolish the plastic house using wrecking balls. Chain saws and torches had to be used to dismantle the reinforced polyester structure, piece by piece. The concrete central foundation still exists and is used as part of a landscaped area directly to the left as you enter Tomorrowland.

Perhaps we should have all listened to Ray Bradbury before removing the House of the Future: "Walt Disney was a dreamer and doer. While the rest of us were talking about the future, he built it. The things he taught us at Disneyland about street planning, crowd movement, comfort, humanity, etc. will influence builders, architects, urban planners for the next century."

WEAR YOUR GUESTS SHOES · PASSION · 3 ORGANI
TY · 9 FOR EVERY OUNCE OF TREATMENT, PI
ON—NEVER STOP LEARNING · 7 TEI
UAL MAGNET) · COLLABOR
KNOW YOUR AUDI
TAKE A C

# COMMANDMENT #10

# KEEP IT UP (MAINTAIN IT)!

As parents, we set the example for our own children. As Disney park hosts, we set the example for millions of children (and adults) around the world every day of the year.

I have watched guests holding trash in their hands, looking for the nearest receptacle to make a deposit. But in the world outside the Disney parks, chances are good that they would not find that trash can, and the deposit they may want to make would end up on the sidewalk or in the street. But Disney parks are so clean that you know at every step that spotless sidewalks, walkways, and streets are no accident.

Without even thinking about it, you do not want to violate your host's standards. So you find that nearby trash can— because the last thing you want is your son or daughter (or your spouse) to see you setting a poor example for them.

For Disney, it's not just the cleanliness of the streets and walkways. It's thousands and thousands of things that work every hour of every day, from the animation of the auctioneer in Pirates of the Caribbean to the plunge of a log flume vehicle at Splash Mountain. If we sat down to list all the items that are expected to work flawlessly and continuously during your visit—air-conditioning systems, elevators, seat belts, vehicle brakes, sound systems, special provisions for disabled guests, and thousands more—we could easily spend our vacation trying to create the list that Disney park and resort maintenance staffs already have computerized, because it's their daily challenge and responsibility.

The cardinal principle is this: when things do not work, your experience as a guest is negatively impacted. Poor maintenance is poor show. And poor show is unacceptable in the Disney experience.

In a Disney park or resort, everything must work. It's not about *us*: it's about *you and your family*.

# And the Mousecar goes to . . .

### The American Adventure maintenance team, Epcot, Walt Disney World

In thinking about the award for this commandment, I discovered a long-forgotten interview I did for the Disney Channel about one of my very favorite attractions: The American Adventure in Epcot.

Maybe it was the lyrical narration in the video—I admired the cadence of actor Lloyd Bridges's speech—and he rightly called the show "one of the most ambitious Disney has ever created." Or perhaps it was the reminder of the six years (and that many failures) it took before we got the show right at Imagineering. (Lesson: don't be afraid to fail. If everything works the first time, you're probably just repeating what you did last time.)

It would be easy for the creative story and engineering teams to take all the credit for this show. I'll get to them later, because they indeed achieved an amazing accomplishment.

But my main focus here is on the incredible Epcot maintenance staff that has kept a show as complicated as any Broadway production as fresh and new as it was on day one in October 1982—more than thirty years ago.

Here are just a few of the challenges they face every day:

- Keeping thirty-five Audio-Animatronics "actors" performing their roles flawlessly, once each hour throughout the day—including their movements, period costuming, and spot-on locations in each scene.
- Making sure the scene changer—a 65-foot-by-35-foot-by-14-foot steel framework weighing 350,000 pounds—is in exact position for each show performance at all times. The scene changer, operated by more than two dozen computers, moves the sets horizontally into place. The sets rise into audience view on telescoping hydraulic supports. There are seven separate lifts carrying the thirteen dimensional sets and thirty-five animated "performers." The scene changer is as long as a railroad boxcar and twice as wide.
- Keeping the rear projection screen—28 feet high by 155 feet long—in perfect focus. At the time of its installation, it was the largest projection screen ever used. Over three thousand feet of seventy-millimeter film are projected on that screen.

Show director Rick Rothschild says this is "the most complicated 'play' we have ever created in our parks—and the first ever with so many Audio-Animatronics 'actors' onstage." But there's one thing missing on the stage: there is no stage. Although the audience in the 1,024-capacity theater cannot see this, the "actors" are supported on small platforms surrounded by open space, wires, and pipes. One other stage standard is also missing: although there is a wardrobe room to store extra costumes, there are no dressing rooms. (In more than thirty years, the Audio-Animatronics actors have not complained even once!)

The success of this complex system is still breathtaking more than three decades later, especially when you read comments like this one from Steve Alcorn, one of the engineers: "To give you an idea of how fluid things were, when we started designing the control system for The American Adventure, we thought the lifts were going to be on a turntable, not a carriage. Yet the building was already under construction."

Most of our original creative team for The American Adventure is gone now: writer-producer Randy Bright, one of the leaders of Epcot show development . . . Walter Tyler, our art director and designer of the sets—Walter won an Academy Award for Best Art Direction for the 1949 epic *Samson and Delilah* and was nominated nine more times for films in the fifties and sixties . . . and Bob Moline, who cowrote the beautiful "Golden Dreams" song with Bright. Fortunately, Rothschild is still show directing (Star Tours, Captain Eo, Soarin', etc.) and has also served a term as president of the international Themed Entertainment Association (TEA).

It's no wonder then, that when I think about the "Keep It Up (Maintain It)!" commandment, my thoughts go to this very special attraction in Epcot. When I visit Epcot, it's always the first place I go for chills, thrills—and just plain admiration for an incredible Disney experience.

# And The Goof goes to . . .

### "Lost Disneyland Maintenance"
### of the early 2000s

In September 1967, Richard Irvine, Imagineering's head of design, asked me to put together a booklet of Walt Disney information. It was less than a year after Walt's passing, and Dick's objective was stated in my cover note for what turned out to be a 127-page book: "The intent here is to provide, as a foundation, Walt's thinking and philosophy as it was applied in Disneyland, and additionally Walt's thoughts about Walt Disney World as they apply to what we are now beginning."

In that "Background and Philosophy" volume, under the heading "Walt's Quotes re: Disneyland," I incorporated twenty-seven individual quotes about Disneyland, including these two:

- On Doing Things Right—"Everybody thinks that park [Disneyland] is a gold mine—but we have had our problems. You've got to work it and know how to handle it. Even trying to keep that park clean is a tremendous expense. And those sharp pencil guys tell you, 'Walt, if we cut down on maintenance, we'd save a lot of money.' But I don't believe in that—it's like any other show on the road; it must be kept clean and fresh."

- On "Keeping the Show on the Road"—"To keep an operation like Disneyland going you have to pour it in there. It's what I call 'Keeping the Show on the Road.' You have to keep throwing it in; you can't sit back and let it ride. Not just new attractions, but keeping it staffed properly . . . you know, never letting your staff get sloppy . . . never let them be unfriendly. That's been our policy all our lives. My brother and I have done that and that is what has built our organization."

As I thought back on the earliest days of Disneyland, when most of the standards related to "Keep It Up (Maintain It)!" were established, several images immediately popped into my memory. The first was a handwritten sign about four inches by eight inches that arrived on the desk of Bill Cottrell, then president of WED Enterprises. The words about a sale in one of the shops leased to outside operators were handwritten in ink marker. Cottrell immediately went to Walt with two issues: we don't have "sales" in Disneyland, and we don't do handwritten Magic Marker signs as though someone had just discovered something they wanted to communicate to guests. Good planning—and good hosting—requires that you have thought these issues out *in advance*—in plenty of time to *print* a well-designed sign communicating your message to guests.

That Magic Marker sign brought the issue to a head. As the designer and standard-bearer of good taste and good design, WED's leaders issued an edict, with Walt's active support: "No more Magic Marker signs—and no sales in

Disneyland." That was sixty years ago, and no one in the Disney Parks and Resorts division questions the importance of this order.

The second image that came to me was that of one of the earliest Disneyland cast members, a "White Wing" street sweeper named Trinidad. The term *white wing* was used early in the twentieth century when referring to a street cleaner, often seen wearing an all-white uniform; his (they were always men) main job was to follow the horses up and down the main streets of America, cleaning up after them.

And with his expertise at wielding his broom and shovel on Disneyland's Main Street, Trinidad Ruiz was a throwback to an earlier age. One day as he worked his magic before the start of a parade, Trinidad realized that the eyes of the guests waiting at the curb for their parade to begin were *on him*. From that moment on, Trinidad realized he was a performer—*onstage*. No one before or since has performed that role with such panache and gusto. Truly, Trinidad Ruiz was a star onstage—on Disneyland's Main Street, U.S.A.

Here's the point: even the most mundane job must be done with skill and enthusiasm to maintain those Disney standards of cleanliness, friendliness, and safety. And if that's your role in the Disneyland show, you do it the best way you know how—with panache and gusto! You must *keep it up*— every day—because that day may be the only day a family from Peoria or Pomona or Paris visits a Disney park.

A little more than ten years ago, in the early part of this new century, these standards were not being met at Disneyland. In my book *Dream It! Do It!*, I detailed the way the management of that time had allowed the park to deteriorate—with peeling paint, rotting wood, and, sad to say, even when it came to addressing several safety issues— all as the park's fiftieth anniversary approached in 2005.

In his excellent book *Disney U* about Disney standards of service, Doug Lipp, former leader of the training program called The Disney University at corporate headquarters in Burbank, included this quote from Walt Disney: "We have to keep 'plussing' our show. If we ever lose them [the guests] it will take ten years to get them back."

Walt had it right, and, fortunately, new leaders arrived at Disneyland who were committed to making things right at the Disneyland Resort. They realized what the fiftieth anniversary would mean to the future—not just the ten years that Walt predicted, but for the next half century. We all knew that the experience our guests would have during the fiftieth celebration—including the appearance and presentation of the park itself, and certainly the handling of any safety issues—would set the tone for years to come. A great experience for our guests during "The Happiest Homecoming on Earth" would influence guest attitude for the foreseeable future.

The new management team at the Disneyland Resort rose to the challenge. The year prior to the July 17, 2005, celebration was one of the most important in the park's history—onstage and backstage. By the time the celebration began, Disneyland had the happiest face it had presented in years, after a year of fix-up to bring it to the highest standards—and therefore highest *respect*—it had earned and enjoyed.

When we look back on the early years of the twenty-first century, we can certainly see that period as an anomaly in the history of Disneyland—totally out of character with the standards that went before and have prevailed since. But when it comes to those standards of "Keep It Up (Maintain It)!" those years serve as a powerful example and warning, so they deserve to receive The Goof award.

CE OF TREATMENT, PROVIDE A TON OF TREAT
STOP LEARNING • I TELL ONE STORY
SUAL MAGNET) • COLLABOR
) • I KNOW YOUR
AIN IDENTIT
EN

# POSTSCRIPT

I can hear the howls of protest now. How could I possibly not include Mystic Manor in Hong Kong, with that creepy musical score by Danny Elfman? What about the Indiana Jones Adventure in Disneyland—the queue is great, but *the ride* in that off-road simulator vehicle is dynamite! How about Ratatouille at Disneyland Paris? Seeing the City of Lights from a dark "rat's-eye view" as the Pixar film becomes a three-dimensional experience is unique! And how could I forget about the Disney Cruise Line? If there ever was a Mousecar winner, the *Dream* and the *Fantasy* are, well, a fantasy dream come true.

And all would be correct. I had a long list of nominations from the creative design, engineering, and construction projects over the last sixty years by the Imagineers around the world.

In fact, how could I not select my very favorite Epcot attraction, the Living with the Land boat tour through the living laboratories of The Land pavilion? As your boat glides past, you see lettuce and tomatoes and an array of exotic vegetables native to various parts of the world growing through controlled environment agriculture—and then that same produce is harvested and served in the Garden Grill restaurant in The Land. It's the only attraction of its kind in any entertainment park—anywhere. Walt's Epcot? Absolutely!

In making my selections, I recalled the time Walt Disney criticized a concept drawing by Herb Ryman for a new attraction. "Well, if you don't like this," the great artist replied, "tell me what you want me to do." Walt's answer: "Just do something people will like!"

And I happen to like all the ones I selected.

# THE ROAD TO IMAGINEERING

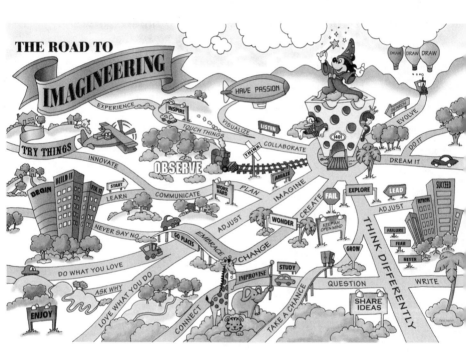

"So you want to be an Imagineer?" writes **Alfredo Ayala**, a twenty-year Imagineer who once told me he was inspired by a book on atomic energy he checked out of his school library when he was in the fifth grade. Now responsible for leading Research & Development project teams that focus on creating innovative technical concepts, Alfredo asks the question of the day—and gives us his answer: "What is an Imagineer in the first place? For me it's a career where art and science coexist and story drives creativity. In a world where parents encourage careers in engineering, law, and medicine, art and other creative careers are discouraged because they are perceived as too risky.

"So if you like to go against traditional thinking," Alfredo continues, "and find yourself always asking 'what if' . . . then you have the spirit of Imagineering in you!"

I've read any number of articles about the interview and hiring practices of successful companies: how to read and decipher a résumé; how to determine whether that portfolio of digital art really belongs to the candidate. But for me, if you were an applicant at Imagineering's door, it is not about whether you went to school at Harvard or MIT or California Institute of the Arts. It's not about your GPA or how you ranked in your class. It's not about where you were born, or what your parents do. It's about you: what's inside your head and heart.

If I get a "yes I do" or "yes I will" answer—if I could see into your head and heart and find most of these words as positive interest and behavior—you would be my next Imagineer.

Now that I've walked you through my essential philosophy about Mickey's Ten Commandments, it's time to start out on The Road to Imagineering. But I wanted that road to be *about us*—the Imagineers—not just about me. Remember that line from Professor Bennis: "None of us is as smart as all of us."

I needed as many Imagineers as possible to participate to make the road about all of us. So I sent this e-mail to about a hundred Imagineers who represent a significant cross section of present and former Imagineers—old and young, technical-minded and artistically talented, university graduates and self-taught individualists, male and female, born in Glendale one mile from Imagineering's headquarters and born across the oceans in far-off lands.

From:  Marty Sklar
To:  Imagineers
Subject:  Preliminary Book 2 Research
Summer 2014

**Background:** I've got the writing bug again! Just getting started!

**Why?** I really loved talking to Disney fans at my presentations and book-signings around the country, and what great interest: 700 in Chicago, 300 in Ocean County, New Jersey, 500 books sold in one day in Old Sacramento, events at Disneyland, Walt Disney World, The Walt Disney Family Museum, The Skirball Museum, etc. There seems to be an insatiable appetite for "more stories"—and so many kids out there who "wanna-be like you!"

**What:** I'm not looking for stories—I can always make them up! What I do want is input from you . . . and information about you!

**The Big Idea:** My goal is to combine an expanded version of my "Mickey's Ten Commandments" with background about Imagineers and your thinking: How you got to those Hallowed Halls, advice about career path, and learning suggestions for those young wanna-be enthusiasts, etc.

**The "Marty Ask":** What I would like is for you to write a paragraph, several paragraphs, or a full page—no more—about what you now know that will help young people who think they want careers in your field. It's an opportunity, I think, to help young people—perhaps to influence their future. I won't promise to use everything or every idea you write, but I will promise to make what I use sound like the author is not writing in Chinese or Japanese! (And please include how you want to be referred to: by profession, job description, title, etc.)

**My Plan:** I have no commitment for the manuscript. I intend to pitch it to Disney Editions in the fall.

**Deadline:** So—I would need your material by September 1.

**About "Book 1":** *Dream It! Do It! My Half-Century Creating Disney's Magic Kingdoms* is doing very well, thank you! It's in its second printing in the USA, about to be published in Japan, with a Chinese edition still to come.

**Thanks for Your Consideration:** You've been giving our fans great fun and entertainment around the world. I think of this project as "giving back." There are lots of folks out there who are waiting for something like this!

\* \* \* \* \* \* \* \* \* \*

I was thrilled with the response: seventy-five e-mails arrived by my deadline from as far away as Shanghai and Paris. Those responses are the foundation for the remainder of this book.

Now I want you to read the words and the thoughts of some of those Imagineers. After all, it's *their* stories of how they became the people they are today that will give you some background and may present an idea, a pathway, a suggestion for you to think about—and perhaps even pursue as your next step.

My role? Well, I think of myself as a kind of ringmaster in a circus of great performers. From my half century at Disney, I know how to bring out the best performances, to make sure that what we are developing (especially in the center ring of major projects) stays on course from a story and design perspective. Most importantly, I had access to all the performers—all the talent representing 140 different disciplines—the same roster of disciplines we put together whenever we create something new for a Disney park or resort around the world.

In keeping with our Ten Commandments theme, I've broken the responses into ten categories. These are the key themes that Imagineers believe are extremely important for their future teammates. Of course there are more, but these ten jumped off the pages I received as recommendations or standards for "wannabes" to learn, understand, and practice. Each section includes a short intro from yours truly and the actual words of the current and former Imagineers.

**STORY**
**PASSION**
**MENTOR**
**COLLABORATION**
**DISNEY PARK EXPERIENCE**
**EDUCATION—NEVER STOP LEARNING**
**BE CURIOUS**

**TAKE A CHANCE / THINK DIFFERENTLY
BECOME THE BEST
IMAGINATIONS**

So many of our values and principles were inspired by Walt Disney's attitude toward the public. "Get a good idea," Walt said, "and stay with it. Dog it, and work at it until it's done, and done right!" Walt's values inspired all of us. Some were very simple, like maintaining a first name place ("The only mister here is Mr. Toad!"). Others were the master storyteller explaining his attitude toward work: "You don't work for a dollar—you work to create and have fun." These foundation values guided our own creative efforts at Walt Disney Imagineering.

We also had the good fortune to work closely with many people in industry, governments, and, of course, the arts around the world. Walt Disney's own visits to the laboratories of great American corporations—GE, IBM, DuPont, RCA's Sarnoff Labs, Westinghouse, and the Bell Labs—inspired his thinking and development of the concept for Epcot as a living community: Experimental Prototype Community of Tomorrow. He was right at home with the people he met because he saw the same creative spark, passions, and collaborative teamwork he had instilled at Disney. Walt saw how their work could, as he said in the Epcot film I wrote, "influence the future of city living for generations to come."

During my Disney career, I was fortunate to get to know, and learn from, a number of international icons who influenced my thinking toward storytelling and our work ethic. One was Ray Bradbury, the great science-fiction writer, poet, and "dreamer of future thoughts." We all know his *Martian*

*Chronicles* and *Fahrenheit 451*, among others. I remember visiting Ray in his West Los Angeles home and seeing his personal philosophy in action: The first thing every morning he was at the typewriter, writing *something*—it didn't matter whether it was a hit or a miss; it was the *discipline* and the *love* of the creative effort that mattered to Ray.

We met Don Hewitt, creator and executive producer of the long-running CBS TV series *60 Minutes*, as we were developing the Epcot park for Walt Disney World. Don was one of the people who shaped our knowledge of world news in America in the second half of the twentieth century. When he retired, he was interviewed on his own program and was asked what his advice was to all the great journalists he directed, including Walter Cronkite, Dan Rather, Mike Wallace, Harry Reasoner, and Diane Sawyer. "My inspiration was the Bible," Hewitt said. "Think about it. The Bible is full of stories that have endured for centuries. So I told our reporters four little words: 'Tell me a story!'"

Those are four little words you can put on my bulletin board any day of the year.

If it sounds as though Shaike Weinberg, founding director of the U.S. Holocaust Memorial Museum in Washington, D.C., and Don Hewitt were singing off the Imagineering song sheet, you are correct. I first met Shaike Weinberg in Tel Aviv, Israel, in 1980 when Imagineering was designing a proposed pavilion for the State of Israel for Epcot. I can still see the exquisite models of Jewish synagogues he had commissioned for display in the Jewish Museum of the Diaspora. Shaike Weinberg was a theater man by background; he saw a museum as a place to tell a story, not just for showing authentic artifacts. He made the architects re-design the

Holocaust Museum so he could have an authentic railroad boxcar to show how Jews and other minorities were transported to the Nazi Concentration Camps. When you visit the Holocaust Museum you will never forget the room full of 4,000 shoes—all that remained of a Jewish community in Poland.

No one works in isolation from the rest of the world, especially in today's world of instant communications and access to information. I learned so many things at the feet of the masters, so to speak, and now am pleased to pass on these values and approaches through the principles on the following pages, beginning, of course, with Story.

NCE OF TREATMENT, PROVIDE A TON OF TREAT
STOP LEARNING • TELL ONE STORY
ISUAL MAGNET) • COLLABOR
TY • I KNOW YOUR
TAIN IDENTI
RIENS

# STORY

For a Disney park, we ask ourselves: is the story repeatable? If it's going to travel around the world, does it work visually? Have we remembered that humor may not translate to other cultures? Above all, we pay attention to the details: in a Disney park, not only is storytelling "the thing"—*every thing tells a story!*

I wanted to start with this note from **Joe Herrington** because he does my job in his own words: introduces himself, explains how he made it on that Road, and how his world has changed over the years:

> *I began as a sound designer when we built Epcot and have had the opportunity to work on every major project since that time. I am now a principal audio media designer, and by the end of this year I will have completed thirty-four fascinating years at Imagineering. That is three decades of living through amazing technological achievements, and in that time*

# Mousecar

Walt created the "Mousecar" (in homage to the Academy Awards' Oscar) to honor "significant contributions" to the company's success.

Roy O. Disney with the first Mousecar.

# The Goof

I asked former Disney animator Joe Lanzisero, Imagineering's portfolio creative leader for Hong Kong Disneyland and Disney Cruise Line projects, to create "The Goof" award "for unfulfilled and underachieved projects."

## COMMANDMENT #1
### Cars Land:
Cars Land at Disney California Adventure.

## COMMANDMENT #2
### Dumbo at Walt Disney World:
Dumbo the Flying Elephant, Fantasyland—Magic Kingdom, Walt Disney World.

## COMMANDMENT #3

### Indiana Jones Queue:

Indiana Jones and the Temple of the Forbidden Eye—Adventureland, Disneyland.

## COMMANDMENT #4

### Fantasyland Castles:

The Fantasyland castles in Disney parks around the world.

## COMMANDMENT #5
### Epcot's World Showcase:
World Showcase in Epcot, Walt Disney World.

## COMMANDMENT #6
### Peter Pan's Flight, Disneyland:
Peter Pan's Flight, Fantasyland, Disneyland.

# COMMANDMENT #7
## Roots of the Carousel of Progress:
Edison Square, Concept for Disneyland, Circa 1957
Inspiration for the Carousel of Progress:
· New York World's Fair, 1964–65
· Disneyland, 1967–1972
· Magic Kingdom, Walt Disney World 1975–Present

**DESCRIPTION**

Edison Square architecturally will be a composite of residential districts of major American cities at the turn of the century. As such, Edison Square will be the residential extension of Main Street in Disneyland, which contains stores, shops and institutional exhibits representative of this same period in American history.

Located just a few steps from Main Street and near the Plaza, the center of Disneyland from which visitors enter each of the "lands," Edison Square will be a paved brick street on which America will be seen passing from the "old" of the 19th Century to the "new" of the early 1900's. The electric light is seen taking the place of gas lamps; horse-drawn vehicles are giving way to electrical and gasoline-powered "horseless carriages."

As they enter Progress Place in Edison Square, where they will find that Progress Is Our Most Important Product, visitors will see two separate plaques on which General Electric's symbol and appropriate words setting forth the theme of Edison Square will appear.

The exterior edifices of Edison Square will include the red brick buildings of Philadelphia, the brownstone of New York City, the graystone of Chicago, wood structures of St. Louis and San Francisco, and the colonial brick of Boston. Inside these buildings, General Electric's theatrical productions will be staged for Disneyland visitors.

Edison Square will be alive and vital. Disneyland's "horseless carriages" and surreys, which travel up and down Main Street, will move in and out of the area. Such annual Disneyland special events as the "horseless carriage" day parade and the Easter Parade will be a part of Edison Square.

The Square itself will be architecturally landscaped befitting the turn of the century. It will contain the "new" electric lamps, iron grill work, hitching posts and other "signs of the times." All the windows in the buildings will be authentically dressed and specially lighted to carry out the atmosphere of the area.

A life-size statue of Thomas A. Edison will be the central landmark of the Square.

# COMMANDMENT #8
## Shanghai Disneyland:
Shanghai Disneyland, aerial photo taken during early construction.

# COMMANDMENT #9
## It's a Small World:

"it's a small world"
· New York World's Fair, 1964–65
· Disneyland Park, 1966
· The Magic Kingdom, 1971
· Tokyo Disneyland, 1983
· Disneyland Paris, 1992
· Hong Kong Disneyland, 2005

# COMMANDMENT #10
## The American Adventure:
The American Adventure, Epcot, Walt Disney World.

In the 1960s, whenever Walt Disney needed a song to capture the spirit of a project, he called on his songwriting team, Robert B. Sherman and Richard M. Sherman. They wrote for motion pictures, TV, attractions at the Disney parks, and the Disney-created shows at the 1964–65 New York World's Fair. They also won two Oscars for *Mary Poppins* (Best Song, " Chim Chim Cher-ee," and Best Original Score).

Walt joined Bob and Dick Sherman to sing the New York World's Fair hit, "There's a Great Big Beautiful Tomorrow," in a short film I wrote as an update to General Electric's Board of Directors.

The animated star of Epcot's Journey into Imagination pavilion, Figment (of the imagination, of course), inspired this verse in Dick and Bob Sherman's "One Little Spark": *"Two tiny wings/ Eyes big and yellow/Horns of a steer/But a loveable fellow/From head to tail he's a royal purple pigment/ And then 'violà!'/You've got a Figment."*

In October 1967, I joined architect Welton Becket (center) and Imagineering chief of design Richard Irvine (right) on the one hundred-acre clearing where the Walt Disney World Magic Kingdom Park would be built. The yellow "X" marks the location of the future Cinderella Castle, which was illustrated by Herbert Ryman.

Maintaining a tradition until his passing, Herbert Ryman drew the very first illustrations of Disneyland, Walt Disney World, Epcot, and Tokyo Disneyland (above).

In October, 2012, Shanghai Disneyland portfolio creative leader Bob Weis and colleagues Jeremy Chaston and John Lindsay (below, left to right) reenacted that 1967 inspirational moment at Walt Disney World on the cleared site in what will be Disney's second park in China. The illustration (left) depicts Shanghai Disneyland's Enchanted Storybook Castle.

Before the opening of Disneyland Paris in 1992, Imagineer Frank Armitage helped introduce the park to Europe and the world with this fanciful storybook illustration.

1 Craig Russell
2 Marty Sklar
3 Bruce Vaughn
4 Owen Yoshino
5 Dorisz Tatar
6 Aileen Kutaka
7 Zofia Kostyrko-Edwards
8 Debbie DelMar
9 Diane Scoglio
10 Bob Gurr
11 Shelby Jiggetts-Tivony
12 Jim Thomas
13 Kevin Rafferty

14 Kathy Mangum
15 Daniel Joseph
16 Eli Erlandson
17 Dave Fisher
18 Susan Zavala
19 Joe Herrington
20 Tom Morris
21 Tim Delaney
22 Dex Tanksley
23 Lanny Smoot
24 Alfredo Ayala
25 Chris Montan
26 Dave Crawford

27 Andy DiGenova
28 Brian Crosby
29 Larry Nikolai
30 Jim Clark
31 Fintan Burke
32 Steve Miller
33 Jess Allen
34 Glenn Barker
35 Eddie Sotto
36 Barry Braverman
37 Josh Gorin
38 Val Usle
39 Marty Kindel

40 Brian Nefsky
41 David Durham
42 Daniel Jue
43 Yves Benyeta
44 Omar Fuentes
45 Chris Runco
46 Kym Murphy
47 Coulter Winn
48 George Scribner
49 John Olsen

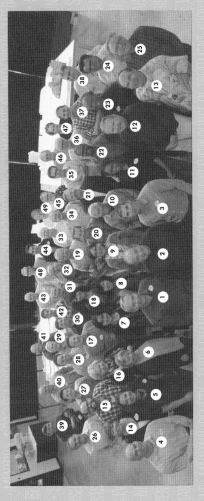

Peggie Fariss and Zsolt Hormay meet in front of Le Château de la Belle au Bois Dormant (Sleeping Beauty Castle) at Disneyland Paris.

With the dramatic Enchanted Storybook Castle as the backdrop, Bob Weis (third from left), the Shanghai Disneyland park's creative leader, joins key teammates (left to right) Gordon Lemke, Doris Hardoon Woodward, Lori Coltrin, Abe Quibin, and Stan Dodd at the construction site.

As a retirement gift, the Florida Imagineers had senior show production designer Tom Rodowsky and art director Joni Van Buren create my favorite character wearing my favorite hat and playing my favorite sport, tennis. The inscription reads: MARTY "ACE" SKLAR—WORLD CHAMPION OF CREATIVITY. THANK YOU FOR INSPIRING US TO PLAY OUR BEST.

Diego Parras, Theron Skees, and Steve "Mouse" Silverstein (left to right) at our Florida office.

When our group photo was taken, landscape designer Paul Comstock was in South America. He sent me an update about his travels and this story about his mentor, Disney Legend Bill Evans, hired by Walt Disney in 1954 to make Disneyland a garden of beautiful trees, plants, and flowers. "I'm in Patagonia," Paul wrote, "on the trail of the Southern Beech trees in their native habitat. During construction of Disneyland Paris in 1991, Bill said, 'We need a tall-growing stately evergreen tree for Town Square.' Bill sent me across The Channel to find *Nothofagus dombeyi*, Southern Beech trees, which had been acquired as trial seedlings from southern Chile by the British agricultural test station at South Hampton in the 1930s. I selected eight trees, forty feet tall, for Town Square, and the spares were planted in Adventureland. Today in southern Chile I finally got to close the loop and experience these magnificent trees in their native habitat!"

"Welcome, foolish mortals . . ." Tom Fitzgerald and I dressed as Disneyland Haunted Mansion hosts for the introduction we wrote for a book about this beloved attraction.

Disney Legends vehicle designer Bob Gurr (center) and composer and lyricist Richard Sherman join me for a reunion at Imagineering.

Disney Legend John Hench and I represented the company at the fifteenth anniversary of Tokyo Disneyland in 1998.

"All Aboard!" for adventure at Hong Kong Disneyland. This train is named in honor of one of Disney's most esteemed presidents, the late Frank G. Wells.

This photo for one of Disney's Annual Reports was taken in front of the Disneyland Opera House, home of Great Moments with Mr. Lincoln.

A warm jacket was required on cool mornings, even in sunny California, during construction of Disney California Adventure.

Construction site of Disney California Adventure, then our ninth, prior to its opening in 2001. Major additions and changes in 2012 introduced Cars Land and the 1930s-era Buena Vista Street.

While studying the size and location of the Epcot pavilions before the park's opening in 1982, we built this model—which was just big enough for midsize people like me to feel like giants!

Some Epcot study models, like this one that I reviewed with designers John DeCuir Jr. (left) and John Hench, were more for "show" presentations to potential pavilion sponsors.

John Hench and I used this Epcot model to inform Disney corporate leaders and major companies about the park's planning and design concepts.

Storyboards are used in concept presentations and in story-development discussions like this one with creative staff members Eric Jacobson (left), Randy Bright (right), and Brock Thorman (behind me).

The Model Shop, which was managed by Bob Sewell (right) in the early days, gave Walt the chance to review designs in three dimensions.

This storyboard review featured costume designs for Hong Kong Disneyland.

Reviewing construction projects with the team is important. Here a review is under way at the Tokyo DisneySea site before the park's opening in 2001.

When we appeared together, John Hench and I could say that, combined, "we have over one hundred years of Disney service." I was "the kid" with only fifty-four years. John's Disney career spanned sixty-four years.

Creative leaders work with many design disciplines. Here I'm reviewing lighting with designers Ann Malmlund and Joe Falzetta.

Our Epcot team included Disney Legends (left to right) Fred Joerger, Orlando Ferrante, John Hench, me, and Collin Campbell.

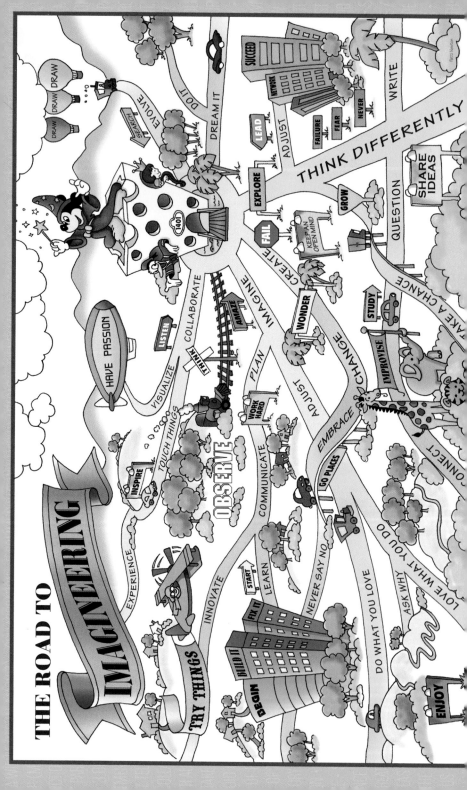

*I have watched technology overtake a generation. Some have come to use it well, while others have let it use them. For them, it is sometimes hard to remember that technology is just one of our many tools. We, the Imagineers, are the master storytellers who must rein technology the way a skilled horseman reins a spirited horse.*

*I was born in Houston, Texas, but immediately moved to the prairie lands of Texas. As a boy, I loved technology, but I came from a background of old west storytellers. So the heart of my job here came to fit like a glove. I schooled at Odessa College and San Diego State University, where I thought I was destined to teach astronomy, or at least some physical science. But my love for technology led me into radio and television, then to film and sound. I settled here in the highly technical field of sound production, but I consider myself a storyteller first and foremost.*

*To pick a favorite project over the years is a difficult task, but a few rise to the surface because the story to be told required that we break new technological ground. Radiator Springs Racers in Disney California Adventure certainly did that. Kevin Rafferty and I were joined at the hip on that one to ensure story, story, story. There was so much brand-new technology in our war bag, but we never let it get in the way of the simplicity of the story to be told. Consequently, our guests don't notice that amazing futuristic technology; rather they joyfully experience the beauty of the story.*

*Similarly, the Indiana Jones story at Disneyland*

*required a vehicle that felt and sounded like a real off-road vehicle. Every move, bump, and turn had to be convincing and in perfect sync with the sound. Nothing existed, so we had to invent something that did the job. With that new technology came a whole new way to write music, create a sound track, and deliver audio. With each new attraction, we add new tools to our storytelling toolbox, but our guests don't notice those cool technological tools. Instead, they are living in our stories, and loving it.*

I've started you on The Road to Imagineering with Joe Herrington's words because I want you to note four key points that you will read over and over again as you travel along this road—and these pages:

1. "I consider myself a storyteller, first and foremost."
2. Embrace change—learn not only to accept, but also to make those amazing technological achievements work for you.
3. The Indiana Jones vehicle: solve a challenge by "inventing something that did the job."
4. Note that technology's role is *in service to story*. As Joe emphasized: "We break new technological ground . . . to ensure story, story, story."

The last word on this comes from **Doris Hardoon Woodward**, senior director/executive producer for the Shanghai Disney Resort project: "Pass on the secret," Doris wrote me: "IT ALL STARTS WITH STORY!"

# PASSION

It's not just about finding something you "like" to do. Explore, try new things, until you find something you *love* to do. Then you have found your *passion*.

> "No one can tell you what to do with your life. But if you are going to dedicate fifty hours a week for thirty to forty years of your life, you need to be doing work that feeds your passion . . . you better love what you do."
>
> **John Dennis,** Music Supervisor

> "So what do you want to be when you grow up? Choose your area of interest and that will affect what classes you take in school, what extracurricular activities you become involved in, what hobbies you choose. . . . And they should all be something you enjoy and are passionate about. If you aren't passionate about the specific work you do, then

you're in the wrong field. Passion isn't a requirement for a job, but it's often what separates the great ones from everyone else."

David Durham, Creative Designers Studio Lead,
Inspirational Blue Sky Program Lead

"Do it for love, not for money, or you will forever be unfulfilled."

Stan Dodd, Executive Producer/Creative Director—
Adventure Isle, Shanghai Disneyland

"I get asked a lot by young people for career advice. The first thing I tell them is that they should explore what they are passionate about and develop that skill."

Kathy Mangum, Portfolio Creative Executive,
Walt Disney World Projects

"The most popular comment I receive at the marvelous Disney fan events is 'My child wants to be an Imagineer.' I'll ask the parents if their boy or girl showed a consuming passion for something creative by age five. I'll also ask if they pursued educational opportunities toward that passion, and how much persistence did they apply to it. I usually get the answer visually from both parent and child. Eyes light up, knowing glances—the absence of which quickly reveals that being an Imagineer is only their dream, not their continuing creative work passion."

Bob Gurr, Disney Legend,
Retired Imagineer Designer

"The first thing is to figure out what your passion is and pursue it. What is it that you love to do, and how does it fit into the Imagineering world? For me it was music, along with the creative and technical aspects of sound. Go to school—learn everything you can about not only your main interest, but other associated interests (photography, magic, cinematography, mechanical devices . . .).

**Glenn Barker,** Principal Media Designer

"Love what you do. *To me, this is more important than 'Do what you love.'* . . . Whatever job you can get, no matter how small or simple, have the passion to do it well."

**Daniel Jue,** Portfolio Creative Executive, Tokyo Disney Resort

"Passion is a key element in my own work, so it's vital to find something to be passionate about. I try to do things that I have not done before, but still leverage things learned from previous assignments."

**Eddie Sotto,** Former Imagineer President of SottoStudios

"My colleagues and I are in it for the love of creating places that people fall in love with, somehow knowing that by creating such places— places that respect and inspire people, positively influence their behavior and reaffirm the best qualities of life—we can influence the world around us. Great spaces become great models for other people to follow."

**Tom Morris,** Executive Creative Director

"Either you're passionate about something or you aren't. I've yet to hear anyone express being semi-passionate about something! The wonderful thing is that when you are naturally passionate about what you are doing, really good things tend to happen because of it!"

**Steve "Mouse" Silverstein,**
Former Imagineer,
Animation Systems Principal Specialist,
Walt Disney World

"First know what you're good at and what your passion is. This is the thing that should wake you up before the alarm clock, keeping you daydreaming and wondering . . . the thing that is burning inside. This passion and pursuit will sustain you through dynamic and fast-paced project environments, where the positive tension between disciplines reaches its peak."

**Theron Skees,** Executive Creative Director

"What do I look for? Passion. We see a lot of résumés, and most of them are impressive. So, how do we choose one talented designer over another? I look for passion. When I am interviewing someone, I want to see them be excited about their work."

**Michael Valentino,**
Principal Show Lighting Designer

*"There are as many ways to get in the door as your imagination can conjure, but they all require passion and persistence. Make a lasting impression with both your portfolio and enthusiasm."*

**Laurence D. Gertz,** Former Imagineer, Creative Director and Producer

ICE OF TREATMENT, PROVIDE A TON OF TREAT
STOP LEARNING • TELL ONE STORY
SUAL MAGNET) • COLLABOR
T) • I KNOW YOUR A
AIN IDENTIT
IENS

# MENTOR

Find someone whose ideas, experience, and advice you think can guide and teach you—not someone you want to "copy," but someone you can learn from, someone you *trust* as a talent, leader, or friend. More than one mentor is perfectly acceptable—and don't be afraid to ask.

*"Don't let your mom decide your future—Mother doesn't always know best. Help others—I've had so many mentors, teachers, angels. I know upon whose shoulders I stand and honor them by helping others as they helped me."*

**Shelby Jiggets-Tivony,**
Creative Development Executive,
Creative Design Studio

*"Growing up in Limerick City, Ireland, during the 1960s, my father would take us on a walk after dinner (dinner was around 1:00 p.m.) on Sundays. By the time we got back home, it was usually freezing cold (especially during the winter), and my father would*

*light a turf fire. This was such a wonderful time for us as we got ready to watch* The Wonderful World of Disney. *Half past five on our black-and-white television would come this amazing man inviting us into his World of Disney. As he held his pointer stick and showed us what was about to unfold in front of us, it inspired us to dream, to dream of another place, to take us to another World to imagine. It was the most wonderful time in a child's life. My father and mother had nine children; we didn't have very much in the way of 'things,' but we had an abundance in imagination. These were the most precious times and never to be forgotten."*

**Fintan Burke,** Technical Director—Principal, Animation

*"I grew up in a house where we were encouraged to become involved in music and the visual arts. I learned to play the piano and drums and was actively involved with the music programs offered in the Arcadia public schools. My mom loved to paint, and studied still life and portraiture. My dad was a serious amateur photographer. I spent many a Saturday night helping him develop and print photos in black and white as well as color. Now, my favorite possessions are portraits of my family by my mom and dad. Today, one of my sisters is a bassoonist with the Los Angeles Philharmonic. While I'm not an expert in any of this, the experience was valuable in that it helped me understand the artistic and professional endeavors of the Imagineers who were."*

**Marty Kindel,** Principal Audio-Video Engineer

"It was very common for seasoned Disney veterans to mentor the new hires most akin to their specialties. Disney Legend Fred Joerger mentored me for two years in the Model Shop, where I learned what the pulse and temperament of Imagineering was and how to apply it to my assignments. Then in 1976 he offered to field-test me on a themed water park assignment at Walt Disney World to see if I would fit the field environment and conditions, which are radically different than the dreamer realm of the Glendale campus. During my lengthy career with Imagineering, I have done my best to carry on the mentoring tradition by working closely with those young Imagineers that worked in my area of focus, Production Design and Field Art Direction of Character Finishes."

**John Olsen,** Retired Imagineer

"I have been interested in science for as long as I can remember. One of my earliest memories is of my father (who was not scientifically trained, but who was always tinkering with electrical and mechanical things) bringing home a push button, a battery, and a bulb. He wired them up, and made the bulb light. Wow, did I ever see the light! From then on, it seems, I have wanted to do technical or scientific things."

**Lanny Smoot,**
Disney Research Fellow

"In all my years at Imagineering, I have been amazed at not only the great things Imagineers get to *work on, but the passion they have to help and teach other people like myself. Along the way, I've had amazing Imagineers teach me many things. But most of all, they made me learn something: always give back. Reaching out and helping people will bring you more satisfaction than anything else you ever do."*

**Diego Parras,**
External Communications Manager,
Walt Disney Imagineering Florida

*"Randy Bright, vice president of Creative and a writer by trade, recognized something in me. He began to compliment my writing, and whenever he asked for my thoughts in a meeting, the floodgates burst open. Randy gave me my first break. I've listened and learned from the masters, paid close attention to my colleagues from all other disciplines, so much that I've learned to think like them, and have come to understand and appreciate what works, what doesn't, and why in the wonderful world of Imagineering. After all that, I think I've finally arrived at a place where I can put all this knowledge and experience together and take on the challenge and profound responsibility of being a creative director. Just yesterday a young Imagineer who has been here for nine months told me she was ready to be a creative director and asked for my advice on how to make that happen. 'Well,' I responded, 'how are you at dusting models?'"*

**Kevin Rafferty,** Executive Creative Director,
Creative Design and Development

"No one gets through this world alone. Outside of work, we have families and friends who support us and help guide us through life. The same is true in the workplace, and it is especially true in creative organizations. As you share your passions, look for people who respond to you. That person may be a good candidate to become a mentor. And just like the family and friends analogy I used earlier, most successful people have more than one mentor. Keep an open mind when you meet new people in and around your work. You have no idea what experiences that person has gone through to get where they are in the organization. Who knows, they may have the one piece of the puzzle you need to move on to the next steps in your career. Do not be shy on this point. It never hurts to ask someone if they will be a mentor or adviser for you. If you approach it correctly, most people will be flattered that you even asked them."

**John Dennis,** Music Supervisor

"As my mentor, Disney Theatrical Vice President John DeSantis, taught me: assume nothing, question everything."

**Gordon Lemke,** Show Design and Production Manager, Shanghai Disneyland

"I got the best overview of Imagineering when I was a coordinator. I was fortunate to work with many of the people (that is: Legends) who started this industry, and since I spent time with them at

*Disneyland on various projects and rehabs, I had time to chat and get a lot of detailed background of the company and heard about their various experiences."*

**Steve Miller,** Retired Director, Project Management

*"Regardless of what your mother told you, you are not the only bright light in that room."*

**Debbie DelMar,** Retired Disney Technology
Executive and Former Imagineer

*"I can trace my passion for the arts back to my parents. Neither of them could draw, but they were both artists in their own right. My dad was an expert storyteller, and my mom embraced any type of art, dance, or music class she could find. Perhaps the best encouragement I received from them was to find what made me happiest and turn that into something I could do for a living. After careful consideration, I realized my brightest dream was to have a career in a field where creativity was highly valued. When it came time to deciding what I wanted to be when I grew up, I knew my choice had to be based on my passion for art."*

**Owen Yoshino,** Creative Director,
Principal Concept Designer,
Tokyo Disneyland Projects

*"At Imagineering, my favorite project was when I worked on the World Showcase and EPCOT Center early in the process. Harper Goff trusted me (very young me) with some of the design of the World*

Showcase. Harper took me under his wing and allowed me to design most of the pavilions for the World Showcase model that he was putting together at the WED Model Shop, which was very educational (research, design presentation, commentaries, and final solutions). After that I worked on the medieval show set for Spaceship Earth, which later was built as I had conceived it. Last, but not least, it was fabulously interesting to be in the story sessions with Ray Bradbury, you, John DeCuir Jr., and others, surrounded by fabulous artwork by Claudio Mazzoli and Jono Lim. I was the fly on the wall, writing the story on index cards to be placed on the wall. I guess I was there because I had very clear penmanship. . . . It was wonderful! I was not 'boxed' into a perception of what architects 'should do.' I was allowed to grow and expand wherever I could and would. WED fed my creative side from every possible angle."

**Eli Erlandson,** Retired Imagineer, Principal Architect

WEAR YOUR GUESTS SHOES • PASSION • 3 ORGANIZE
9 FOR EVERY OUNCE OF TREATMENT, PRO
ON—NEVER STOP LEARNING • 7 TELL
UAL MAGNET) • COLLABORA
KNOW YOUR AUDIEN
TAKE A CHA
CE

# COLLABORATION

There's a reason that sixty years later, there's still only one name on the door at *Walt Disney* Imagineering. The Imagineers are the definition of a **TEAM** whose creations are the joint venture of many creative minds and talents. They *collaborate*!

> *"In my opinion, the unwritten rule of Imagineering is Being a Part of a Family. A family where everyone's ideas count; regardless of whether we think it is valid at that moment or not, it still counts. Growing up in Hungary, I had been taught as a young man 'more eyes see more,' and furthermore, I believe more minds think more. That is the essence of Imagineering. It is not based on individuality and self-recognition; it is based on everyone striving together as a team to solve impossibilities. That is what puts Imagineering on top of any list in the industry. 'Impossible' is not in our vocabulary."*
> **Zsolt Hormay,** Vice President, Creative

"I have learned so many valuable things from my colleagues here at WDI over the years. In doing this, I have gained many lifelong friends at Imagineering. I ask myself why is this, why can I come up with half an idea in a brainstorm and have someone in the seat next to me finish my thoughts in perfect harmony? This is because so many of these wonderfully creative and interesting people have a similar story to mine. We all were children who looked at the world in a different way, an unconventional way, but not a bad way. It is through art, design, and engineering that we express ourselves, and at Walt Disney Imagineering, that is the only way to see the world!"

**Daniel Joseph,** Senior Special Effects and Illusions Designer

"Stressing the importance of teamwork is critical to understand. If the artist is working on an illustration, an art director can change it and even draw on your work. This is sometimes hard to handle for artists. You must get used to it, always keeping in mind your work is part of the whole."

**Maggie Elliott,** Retired Senior Vice President, Creative Development Administration and Head of Model Shop

"Whenever I had a choice, I chose to work with a team that I never had worked with before in order to learn new methods and new ways of leading. The result was that I gained much more experience by exposing myself to new people, and more people were exposed to me."

**Daniel Jue,** Portfolio Creative Executive, Tokyo Disney Resort

"What we do at Imagineering is a collaboration of many disciplines. Be ready to work with others having diverse skills and viewpoints. The ability to communicate verbally and in writing is important, but it is also important to be an active listener. Learn to stand up for the things that are important to you, but be ready to find alternate solutions to solve a problem."

**Marty Kindel,** Principal Audio-Video Engineer

"Having a skill is important, of course, but another vital component of working here is the ability to work inside a team structure. It doesn't matter if you're the most talented engineer or artist ever—if you can't work well with others, you won't succeed here. Our projects are complex and require a huge team to deliver them. If people don't want to work with you, you won't be placed on teams or given assignments. I try to tell people not to underestimate the importance of likability—it's as important as technical skills. This is squishy and isn't taught in schools; it's not something that is easily identifiable on a résumé or in an interview, so sometimes we don't know if a person can work within our environment until they

*get here. I've seen people crash and burn here for*
*the simple reason that they forget whose name is on*
*the front door."*

**Kathy Mangum,** Portfolio Creative Executive,
Walt Disney World Projects

*"If you have a big ego, I suggest you look*
*elsewhere. Disney is always a team effort and*
*individual recognition is rare. Recognize that all of*
*your great ideas will probably end up in a drawer and*
*not in a theme park."*

**Gordon Lemke,** Show Design and Production Manager,
Shanghai Disneyland

*"Teams win the war: one of the first things I*
*realized about WED/Imagineering was that I needed*
*to recognize the staggering wealth of talent that was*
*available. Not just artists, but talent in virtually every*
*discipline from engineers to writers to accountants.*
*And more importantly, it was these people who*
*collectively won the complicated wars of creative*
*effort that eventually brought to life the miraculous*
*Disney projects that are enjoyed by people around*
*the world. What an honor."*

**Kym Murphy,** Retired Imagineer
Producer/Project Manager,
The Seas in Epcot, Walt Disney World

*"I call it* Additive Collaboration. *It's not enough*
*to simply collaborate, for you could do that by*
*holding your nose and grudgingly going with the flow*

because you were told to, or because there's no other choice. Buzz Price (economic adviser to Walt Disney and former chairman of CalArts) spoke often about 'yes IF' enablement, and improvisational theater has long taught us the importance of 'yes AND' contributions. That is what additive collaboration is about: not being afraid to make someone else's idea work or to enhance an idea of your own by incorporating others' ideas and designs into it. A personal example is what happened to me when I was directing the design of the castle for Disneyland Paris. After personally completing the design for the main tower, about which I was very self-congratulatory, I showed it to my colleague Ed Sotto, who was directing the creative efforts for Main Street, just to get feedback (and, really, to only hear 'great job' and nothing else). His feedback was 'Looks great, but have you considered making the arches under the balcony look like tree branches?' (This was a motif being used elsewhere on the castle.) It would have been easy to say 'yes, but' or 'no, this' (or 'mine, mine . . .'), but I had to admit it was a great idea and immediately incorporated it . . . because it was the best thing for the overall design and guest experience."

**Tom Morris,** Executive Creative Director

"Project managers must listen to all desires, proposals, and all perspectives but hold the authority to make decisions through collaboration with creative partners and the project core team in the overall best interest of the project. Every problem has a solution. You're not (and don't have to be) the smartest person on your project team. Leverage the collective talent and expertise of your teams to get to the solution. Respect the talents and skills of your fellow Imagineers and trust them to act responsibly."

**Jim Thomas,** Retired Senior Vice President, Project Management

"Imagineering is a special place because so many talented people from so many different disciplines and backgrounds come together to create these incredibly complex, huge things. A key to success is learning how to work with people who don't think and communicate like you do. That means engineers partnering with creative designers, show writers with programmers, and so much more. Find opportunities to work on projects with people different from yourself—whether they come from a different discipline, culture, or even industry. Try to see things through the eyes of others. Often the fresh mix of perspectives will ignite new ideas you didn't even think possible, and you'll wind up with a whole greater than the sum of its parts."

**Josh Gorin,** Creative Director, Experience Design and Integration, Research and Development

"Collaboration is one of the best forms of creativity for me. I find that putting our heads together invites new thoughts and ideas into the open. We come to a

*place together that we would not get to individually.
I have to say that the best thing about Imagineering
is the people who work here. Working as a group,
designing with the same vision, telling the same story
together is exceptionally satisfying. Get practice
working on a project together with friends—seek out
a way to collaborate with others, share ideas, and
learn what the power of many brains can do."*

**Lori Coltrin,** Executive Creative Director,
Fantasyland—Shanghai Disneyland

*"Being part of a team, collaborating, and sharing
ideas with other professionals has been one of the
most fulfilling aspects of being an Imagineer. One of
the most important and difficult lessons to embrace
was to leave my own ego at the door; there is only
one name on it."*

**Jess Allen,** Professional Photographer

*"I learned I would do well professionally if my team
was successful. Think about your own performance
certainly, but reach out to help everyone else on the
team succeed at their job, too. In any team system,
being a collaborative and supportive team member
goes a really long way."*

**Cory Sewelson,** Artist and Designer

NCE OF TREATMENT, PROVIDE A TON OF TREAT
STOP LEARNING • TELL ONE STORY
SUAL MAGNET) • COLLABOR
T • I KNOW YOUR A
AIN IDENTIT
IEN

# DISNEY PARK EXPERIENCE

"Learn by doing." The experience of working in a Disney park or resort creates "teachable moments" that no book or classroom can duplicate. Dealing with the public, observing their reactions, watching them "play"—these are priceless learning experiences.

For many Imagineers, a key beginning to their Disney career was the "frontline" learning they experienced by working in a Disney park or resort.

*"To get my foot in the door with Walt Disney Productions, I applied for a job at Disneyland in 1974. During my interview I was asked what I wanted to do job-wise. By then I had one year of art classes under my belt, so I told my interviewer I wanted to be an artist here, and fantasized that she'd put me in a nice office with a nice window next to legendary Disneyland artist Chuck Boyer. She put me in the dish room at the Plaza Inn restaurant. 'Well, Son,' my dad reassured me, 'the only time you're going to find*

*success before work is in the dictionary.' I worked my tail off in that dish room."*

**Kevin Rafferty,** Executive Creative Director, Creative Design and Development

*"The value of in-park experience. There is nothing that compares with this for gaining knowledge about the environment in which a designer will be expected to work. Theme parks are unique entertainment venues that must withstand the press and contact of literally millions of guests per year. Things wear out quickly under this onslaught, and we have to be able to balance show value and the maintenance that will be necessary to preserve the artistic vision. It doesn't matter which park one has worked in or even which division it was in—I myself worked for seven years at Six Flags Magic Mountain, and it was an invaluable experience to be working directly onstage with the guests."*

**Larry Nikolai,** Creative Director

*"I applied for a summer job at Disneyland after my first year of college, aiming to be a ride operator or merchandise clerk. Instead, the recruiter told me they needed portrait artists on Main Street, and asked me if I could do that. I had not really done many portraits before, except caricatures of friends, but I said yes. Then I went back to my college dorm and madly sketched everyone, to figure out how to do it before the Disneyland Art Festival supervisor reviewed my portfolio two weeks later. I fortunately got the job, and then spent eight hours a day, all summer,*

sketching the guests—the best life-drawing class one could ever have!"

**Chris Runco,** Concept Designer

"Suddenly the future was clear and simple—become an architect and help build Walt's vision. Education aligned with the vision and led to architecture school. With parents well aware of the passion, it was not long before I heard my father's advice: 'You want to work for Disney? Go get a job at Disneyland.' That led to three years of driving the Monorail, and as graduation approached, WED posted an entry-level position at the park for a research analyst to work on Epcot. The associated job interview was the final domino to move in June of '78, and later that month, over the course of a single weekend, diploma was received on Saturday, Monorail was driven for the last time on Sunday, and a new Imagineer started at 1401 Flower Street on Monday."

**Val Usle,** Sustainability Design Executive

"I worked in the Disney parks: five years at Walt Disney World (my first job was washing trays in the dish room of the Soundstage Restaurant at Disney's Hollywood Studios) and two years at Disneyland. While in the parks, I served fast food, wiped down tables, hosted attractions, conducted guided tours, and listened to compliments and complaints with a smile from guests on both coasts. I learned what the guests want, and what they don't want, firsthand."

**Jim Clark,** Show Producer

"When I graduated from college, I decided that the best thing to do was to get a business degree and try and get a job working for Disney in some capacity. I took an entry-level job at the Contemporary Resort front desk, at Walt Disney World, which was a great way to learn how Disney operates resorts and theme parks. I learned so much over the three years I worked there, but eventually I applied for a job in the research and planning department at WED Enterprises in California."

**John Verity,** Retired Imagineering Vice President, Tokyo Disney Resort

"I started as a busboy at Disneyland in 1969, then transferred to WED in 1975. Learn to network. This is how I got hired at WED. I helped someone with their project to get hired here and they returned the favor by recommending me. Herb Ryman told me once how he loved doing things for others and was amazed how many good things came back around, often from some other direction. It works; try it."

**Glenn Barker,** Principal Media Designer

"One of the biggest lessons I have learned is a simple one: there is no right way to become an Imagineer. In fact, I have yet to find two Imagineers with the same story of how they got here. As someone who started in a gift shop at Walt Disney World, became a Jungle Cruise skipper, performer, manager, recruiter, entered WDI in HR, and parlayed that into a position in Creative, I'm not even sure I *understand it. My point is this: you can have a plan and a destination, but the reality is that things rarely go according to plan. It's going to evolve, change, and take turns you never saw coming."*

**Andy DiGenova,** Creative Program Manager

WEAR YOUR GUESTS' SHOES • PASSION • 3 ORGANIZ
Y • 9 FOR EVERY OUNCE OF TREATMENT, PR
ION—NEVER STOP LEARNING • 7 TEL
AL MAGNET) • COLLABOR
KNOW YOUR AUDIE
TAKE A CH

# EDUCATION—NEVER STOP LEARNING

We're so lucky in our chosen profession—we learn something new with every new assignment. The opportunity to grow in our field with each new challenge is exciting! We learn by doing, by association with other talents, by trying and failing . . . discovering new ways to create and design our stories. Never stop learning!

Walt Disney set a standard for all who followed at Disney with his example of the importance of learning in our work. There was always access to research to obtain or verify information for films, television, consumer products, publications, and the parks and resorts. And travel: our design team for Disney's Animal Kingdom made a dozen trips to Africa and Asia to study animals in their native habitats—all reflected in the character of the Kilimanjaro Safaris, Harambe village, and other features that make this Disney park so authentic.

At Imagineering, employees are encouraged to pass on their knowledge and experience. Many artists, designers, engineers, and other talents have become teachers, often volunteering their own time to students at California Institute of the Arts (the school of all the arts founded by Walt Disney), Art Center College of Design, the University of Central Florida, and other institutions.

For the past twelve years, Imagineering's chief creative executive, Bruce Vaughn, has served as an adjunct professor in the School of Theater, Film and Television at UCLA. His course, featuring guest lectures by key Imagineers, is called "Disney Theme Parks: The Art and Process of Entertainment Design."

Inspired by this program, Michael Jung, creative executive for theatrical development, began a core curriculum in "Themed and Immersive Experience and Design" at CalArts—his alma mater. "We established a program entitled 'The CalArts Educational Initiative,' in which sixteen master students are invited to participate in a month-long intensive program where they are provided with mentors and given a unique design challenge culminating in a presentation to senior executives at Imagineering," says Jung. "Many of the students were able to garner internships, or even positions within the company, bringing diverse new perspectives to our form."

Michael calls attention to Walt Disney's stated objectives for CalArts: "What young artists need is a school where they can learn a variety of skills, a place where there is cross-pollination. The remarkable thing that's taking place in almost every field of endeavor is an accelerating rate of dynamic growth and change. The arts, which have historically sym-bolized the advance of human progress, must match this growth if they are going to maintain their value in and influ-ence on society."

*"Always keep learning. Do this by reading books, magazines, blogs, attending conferences, etc. Travel as much as you can. It is a humbling and inspiring experience to learn just how much you don't know."*
**Yves Benyeta,** Executive Creative Director

*"Follow a path that you are personally good at and excited about. It's important to love what you're studying and working on once you graduate. No matter which path you take, understanding some of the fundamentals of layout, design, and storytelling is helpful. We deal with real, physical environments. Understanding the basics of organizing a physical space to look good and tell a story is a prerequisite to almost any job in this industry."*
**Dave Crawford,** Executive—Research
and Development Imagineer

*"Never Stop Learning: To understand that there is always something new to learn requires a sufficient level of humility, curiosity, and patience. You must believe that listening is more important than speaking. Constant learning can make you diverse and may give you a valued skill."*
**Daniel Jue,** Portfolio Creative Executive,
Tokyo Disney Resort

"Any form of engineering requires an understanding of the laws of physics and application of mathematics. These can be learned through formal education and practical experience. On the formal side I would encourage a college education in the physical disciplines—electronics, physics, mechanical (applicable to acoustical engineering). In addition, classes about the human vision and auditory systems are valuable. Be sure to augment your knowledge with allied arts activity, such as playing a ukulele, singing in a choir, or attending a local symphony orchestra concert."

**Nelson Meacham,** Retired Imagineer,
Audio/Video Engineering

"My thoughts for wannabe enthusiasts are: complete your education—it will help you be well rounded, bringing a range of thought and experience to your work; learn and develop your craft—knowing how to do your work well is important; and take criticism so that you can improve."

**Omar Fuentes,** Production Coordination

"A lot of students want to come to WDI straight out of school. I didn't, and I would recommend others don't, either. What we do here is specialized. Experience in the broader practice can be very beneficial and make you more valuable when you do join WDI."

**Coulter Winn,** Retired Architecture Executive

"Come in eager to learn. Bring in new ideas, but maintain a strong respect for those who have gone before. The best partnership is one where we can all learn from each other."

**Glenn Barker,** Principal Media Designer

"I never had a choice. I knew from my college days that I would be in music, as a songwriter, player, producer, and singer. What I didn't know was that I would come to Disney and oversee the music development of hundreds of films, animated and live action, Broadway productions, and theme park attractions. And what I learned was that everything that I worked on as a musician before coming to Disney gave me some part of the puzzle that I could use to solve our musical challenges. I think the most important attribute to be successful in the arts (and you hear this a lot) is to be passionate about the field you have chosen. Never stop learning or feel as if you have mastered your medium, because there are always ten new things to learn. And if you can communicate your passion for excellence to your collaborators, you create the best environment for these artists to do their best work."

**Chris Montan,** President, Walt Disney Music

"Growing up in Brazil, surrounded by many cultures, gave me the opportunity to learn many languages: German (our maid was of German descent), Russian (our neighbors were Russian),

Portuguese (my native language), Bulgarian (my parents' native language), Latin (required in school). After our small family of four immigrated to the USA, I learned English, French, Italian, and a little bit of Spanish. . . . In architecture, it is also important to know art and architectural history and corresponding details. The details are what tell the story of the environments we create. WDI architects never stop researching and learning; that is how we feed our minds with inspirational imagery."

**Eli Erlandson,** Retired Imagineer, Principal Architect


"Stay hungry for all knowledge once you know what you want to do for a career. Discover the many ways your gift/talent can be transformed into a career and how that career connects with other fields of study. You may find yourself here at Walt Disney Imagineering!"

**Dex Tanksley,** Principal Facility Designer, Architecture Design Studio

WEAR YOUR GUESTS SHOES • PASSION • 3 ORGANIZE
ITY • 9 FOR EVERY OUNCE OF TREATMENT, PRO
ION—NEVER STOP LEARNING • 7 TELL
UAL MAGNET) • COLLABORA
KNOW YOUR AUDIEN
TAKE A CH
CR

# BE CURIOUS

When you ask "why" or "what if," you have an inquisitive mind that can lead to new directions and discoveries. Be eager to know and try more: *be curious!*

*"If you want to get really good in my field, you should become an insatiable culture vulture and a creative sponge soaking up the world around you. Be curious and open to every subject, detail, location, and experience you come across. Notice and remember, write, shoot, record, or sketch out what captures you any way you can."*

**Zofia Kostyrko-Edwards,** Former Imagineer,
Conceptual Designer and Art Director
Principal, deZign sKape L.L.C.

"Be curious/seek knowledge. *Learning and discovery are lifelong adventures."*

**Tim Delaney,** Former Imagineer,
Principal, Tim J. Delaney Design

*"People expect you to be curious when you are young, and yet young people will not ask questions for fear of looking inexperienced or stupid. Be curious at all ages and stages. Ask away, but also do your homework so you aren't asking nonsensical things."*

**Debbie DelMar,** Retired Disney Technology Executive and Former Imagineer

*"Be inquisitive—it fuels creativity and greatness; be a sponge. The best reward for journeying from here to there is discovering what lies between."*

**Stan Dodd,** Executive Producer/Creative Director—Adventure Isle, Shanghai Disneyland

*"Being an Imagineer is more than a job; it's who you are. You never clock out or disconnect. You're always observing the world around you, imagining how it could be better or how you can entertain people in new ways. You're fascinated by stories in all their forms, and you long to let people live out those stories."*

**Brian Crosby,** Creative Designer

*"One of the things that has helped me more than anything in my career is curiosity. Being curious about your life is invaluable. If you stay curious, you will always be looking at the world that exists and asking how or why this or that came to be. Also, you will look for worlds that don't exist and ask how those could come to be. This gives you an advantage in that you will never fail to try something new. Many times I have seen people*

*miss an opportunity because they were not curious. Curious people find problems interesting. Non-curious people just see them as problems. In highly collaborative and creative workplaces, like Imagineering, being curious will serve you well. Curiosity favors collaboration, and when it comes to solving a tough problem, two heads are better than one."*

**John Dennis,** Music Supervisor

*"Listen: one of the most important aspects of my job as a librarian is to* listen. *I never assume that I know what they want—many times, they do not know what they want or they have been told to draw up a concept, and they are still sorting the concept in their mind. And sometimes by talking they figure it out themselves. It's artistic free association."*

**Aileen Kutaka,** Imagineering Librarian

*"Explore widely and deeply. Keep a close eye on trends in the leisure landscape, but also look beyond entertainment to any realm where audiences are engaged by storytelling and placemaking. Stay abreast of new technology, but don't ignore the enduring forms of human expression that transcend the latest tools and toys. Remain curious and welcome interesting ideas from all sources."*

**Barry Braverman,** Former Imagineer—
Creative Executive

*"There's a big difference between being an Imagineer and doing Imagineering work. The*

best way to understand the kind of person who does Imagineering work is to look at two primary requisites: curiosity and persistence. Walt Disney, and most of the Imagineers I worked with starting sixty years ago, had both of these traits. Remember, the great Imagineers never attended any class entitled 'Disneyland 101.' They figured it out as they went, doing their own search for answers, not waiting for a process or instructions. That method still continues today. When a parent or child recognizes this truth, they might have the right stuff for work as a future Imagineer."

**Bob Gurr,** Disney Legend, Retired Imagineer Designer

"When working with senior management on presentations, I'd listen to what kind of imagery they were asking for and why it was so important to fit it into a specific part of their presentation. It wasn't just words explaining what the photograph was supposed to represent; it was showing what made the architecture, lighting, signage, interior and exterior design, attractions, shops, restaurants, etc.—the whole story line—so magical!"

**Diane Scoglio,** Design Asset Specialist

"Change is constant and can be one of the most exhilarating experiences of your life. Walt Disney would have been the first to tell you to 'be curious about everything. . . .' So always ask questions, try and look at the ordinary and familiar in new, cutting-edge, and inventive ways. Seek out the best in people and be willing to join many teams. Never give up on yourself, and go easy if you have impatience. Never stop learning and have a good attitude while you are."

**Susan Zavala,** Design Asset Specialist

"Walt's 'Four C's'—Curiosity, Confidence, Courage, and Constancy—have been an inspiration for me throughout my years with Disney. In particular, I would have to say that curiosity has definitely shaped much of my career.

"Imagineering is a wonderful place for a person who is insatiably curious. Each day, I did my work assignment in the Model Shop and learned something new from the veterans there. But I would also take every opportunity to look around our facilities and see what else was being designed: the latest blueprints in architecture, new sign concepts in graphics, the ride mock-ups, the maquettes in the Sculpture Shop, critters getting furred in Figure Finishing, machinists putting together the latest Animatronics, etc. One unforgettable example was the day I got to look over the shoulder of my idol, Marc Davis, at his drawing table, as he patiently demonstrated and explained his drawing techniques. Wow!"

**Chris Runco,** Concept Designer

"The most successful Imagineers are those who see 'this is new to me' as an opportunity, not a barrier. They are willing to go outside their comfort zone in the interest of expanding their horizons and gaining new perspectives. We've had Imagineers train as ride operators in the park before designing a new attraction, get certified as playground safety inspectors to design an in-queue play area for kids, and even take cooking classes before designing a restaurant. Constantly ask questions, learn how things work, try new and exciting things, and you'll build up a strong base of experiences and an ongoing curiosity that will serve you well at WDI and in life."

**Josh Gorin,** Creative Director,
Experience Design and Integration,
Research and Development

"Practice constructive curiosity. The best example I can think of is how I fell in love with architecture. My first love, music composition, led me to discover how fundamentally connected it was to architecture. I connected the dots between music and architecture through extrapolating rhythm, melody, pattern, and structure that were common between them. Once I discovered how these two things were connected, I began looking at the world differently. I practice this constructive curiosity every day at WDI, and it continues to provide great benefit to my project teams."

**Dex Tanksley,** Principal Facility Designer,
Architecture Design Studio

WEAR YOUR GUESTS SHOES · PASSION · 3 ORGANIZ
TY · 9 FOR EVERY OUNCE OF TREATMENT, PR
ON—NEVER STOP LEARNING · 7 TELL
UAL MAGNET) · COLLABOR
KNOW YOUR AUDIE
TAKE A CH

# TAKE A CHANCE / THINK DIFFERENTLY

At Disney, we are the heirs to a great legacy of risk taking. From the creation of the first animated feature film, to a new kind of family amusement enterprise, to the purchase of Pixar—Disney has led the entertainment industry by "thinking differently" and taking a chance on new opportunities. Try it—you'll like it!

"I would tell my younger self that you should risk more. You should be less afraid of failure and try more things. You should, as Nike says, Just Do It. Often we are our own worst obstacles. We convince ourselves that we should wait a little while until we have more information, or wait until we get permission, or wait until we're one hundred percent sure, or wait until . . .

"We end up waiting so long that we miss our opportunities. The Boy Scout motto is 'Be prepared.'

Are you prepared? If the opportunity to work at Imagineering was dropped in your lap right this second, are you prepared? Stop saying why you can't and Just Do It!"

**David Durham,** Creative Designers Studio Lead, Inspirational Blue Sky Program Lead

"Working in the landscape architecture field allows me the freedom to 'Create the Physical World' that surrounds us—but there is always a price for creative license. The person who wants to create unique Imagineering landscapes must be able to comprehend the 'ethos and epistemology' of creativity in a corporate structure.

"You must be willing to fly: the 'true heart' creator must be willing to fly . . . and must have no fear to go to the edge and jump. . . . Imagineering is a creative place where there are no safety nets allowed, and one must have a thick skin to take criticism, and have no fear of alienation from those with differing points of view."

**Paul Comstock,** Former Imagineer, Landscape Designer, Principal, Comstock Landscape Architecture, Inc.

"Don't be afraid of the unknown—seek it out! Cherish fate's twists and turns and revel in adventure's mysteries with those brave enough to travel alongside."

**Stan Dodd,** Executive Producer/Creative Director— Adventure Isle, Shanghai Disneyland

"Stay open to new experiences and take the path that will offer the most challenge and opportunity for growth."

**Michael Jung,** Creative Executive—
Theatrical Development

"The most successful Imagineers are those who dare to be daring, to expose themselves, to ask questions, to fail. Failure is good when you learn from it, and then you pick yourself up and move forward a little wiser. For me, living outside my introverted comfort zone became the norm."

**Eli Erlandson,** Retired Imagineer, Principal Architect

"Take any job in any firm to get started. Find seasoned vets to mentor you. Be humble, eager, drink it all in, but do what is necessary to solve the assignment of the day. Be willing to work early, late, anytime, anywhere. Be willing to work on the smallest of tasks in the projects to prove your worth. Learn from everyone you meet. Learn from guests, spend lots of time in the park as a guest (not as a VIP). Work on international projects to understand the international business."

**George Head,** Former Imagineer,
Teacher at Savannah College of Art and Design (SCAD)

# BECOME THE BEST

By definition, everyone on the team cannot be "the best"—but we can all try! And what a thrill it is when each of us strives for the highest quality, the best way, true excellence in our work—and we all become *part of "the best"*!

*"When you do your job with passion, you will excel and you will become the best at what you do. People want to work with people who love what they do. They will want you on their team; they will mentor you; they will give you opportunities. If you take advantage of enough of these opportunities, then someday you may have the luxury to do what you love."*

**Daniel Jue**, Portfolio Creative Executive, Tokyo Disney Resort

*"My advice to you would be to become the best at what you love to do. Many people dilute their expertise by trying to learn some of everything, and I think this weakens their résumé and application, since they're good at a lot of things . . . but not the best at anything. Not to say you shouldn't explore other creative hobbies and interests . . . but we're looking for the best people in the disciplines we're hiring for. It also helps to get as much hands-on experience as possible, work opportunities and internships with other companies in the theme park industry, and to broaden your skill set and interests with creative endeavors, technical projects, and even travel. The more experiences you have, the more you'll have to draw on when trying to solve complex problems."*

**Dave Crawford,**
Executive—Research and Development

*"Everyone has dreams. Don't be afraid to dream big. Our Creator made each of us different, with the ability to succeed in the area or areas where our talents and gifts lie. Follow your dreams, aim high, and enjoy the journey. Life is an E-ticket ride! . . . Which in 'Disney-Speak' means the best! Enjoy it!"*
**Tom Rodowsky,** Senior Show Production Designer,
Walt Disney Imagineering Florida

*"Expanding on the theme of the famous proverb 'Anything worth doing is worth doing well,' I believe that one of the major keys to happiness and success in life is that you should first, in order: 1) discover*

*what it is you love doing most of all, and then 2) spend the rest of your life working toward being the best you can be at doing it. Whether your dream is to become a Disney Imagineer, jazz saxophone player, writer, painter, doctor, or whatever it happens to be, I believe that this same path to happiness, fulfillment, and satisfaction with your life applies equally well. And don't be surprised if along the way you discover totally new and different things that you are even more interested in compared with what you were originally pursuing. That is just part of the wonderfully unpredictable process of discovering what it is that you really love to do most and then doing your very best at it!"*

**Steve "Mouse" Silverstein,** Former Imagineer,
Animation Systems Principal Specialist,
Walt Disney World

*"No matter how difficult something may seem, when you're asked to do it, just say yes, then go figure it out. My experience has been that the people who say yes stay employed. They're generally more positive and optimistic about life in general, and they're more of a pleasure to be around. If you have a passion for Photoshop, learn After Effects; if you love After Effects, learn Maya. If you love Maya, I'm very impressed. Have a passion for something, but be willing to learn and don't argue. Just nod. You'll have plenty of time for arguing when you're managing the company."*

**George Scribner,** Former Imagineer,
Animation Director and Concept Artist

"When I am looking to hire a new lighting designer, I want the best designer I can find. So I tell them to choose a field that they want to spend the rest of their life working in and then become the best in that field. And here is something most people don't know or don't think about: at WDI, we sell to ourselves all of the time. When we have an idea for an attraction, we have to sell the idea to corporate management in order to get the funding to build it. That's called pitching. We pitch an idea for a ride or a show. Here is the funny thing: we have to pitch, or sell to ourselves, all of the time. Late in life I learned a very important lesson—you have to learn to sell yourself. Even though I have worked at WDI for many years and have a large body of work with the company, I still have to sell myself to each new project team."

**Michael Valentino,** Principal Show Lighting Designer

"When opportunities arise, do the job that is asked of you with all the energy and skill you can muster. Offer suggestions, or even alternatives, but first demonstrate competence in the task you were asked to accomplish. Approach each assignment as the most important you will ever have. Make your superiors look good by the quality of your workload and they will notice you. It is quite likely that the first job you get in your chosen field will not be the ultimate job of your dreams. That you will need time to grow into."

**Laurence D. Gertz,** Former Imagineer,
Creative Director and Producer

"You must take responsibility for your career. You must be ready, at a moment's notice, to demonstrate your craft, maybe at the airport waiting to board a plane with a producer standing in front of you. Your commitment to your career must be so complete that your antenna is always up, searching for the next opportunity. You are in full control, meaning you can't abdicate your responsibilities to someone else. You are the one who will make things happen. You are the one most committed to your career. You are always the one who initiates what direction your career will take. It's a great responsibility to the one person you can't deceive or cheat: yourself."

**Brian Nefsky,** Casting Director

# IMAGINATIONS

That "One Little Spark" by Richard M. and Robert B. Sherman says it all:

> *One Little Spark*
> *Of inspiration*
> *Is at the heart*
> *Of all creation*
> *Right at the start of everything that's new*
> *One little spark*
> *Lights up for you!*

Over twenty years ago, in 1992 to be exact, I started a program at Walt Disney Imagineering that intentionally borrowed its name from a real word. We called it ImagiNations. Here's the way it's described today:

> *ImagiNations is a design competition created*
> *and sponsored by Walt Disney Imagineering with*

*the purpose of seeking out and nurturing the next generation of diverse Imagineers. Started in 1992 by Disney Legend and Imagineering executive Marty Sklar, the program has grown to include a separate version sponsored by Hong Kong Disneyland.*

*Throughout the years, hundreds of students from universities all across the United States have participated in this competition and had the opportunity to present their projects to Imagineering executives. Furthermore, many of them have become interns and fulfilled their dream of working alongside Imagineers and seeing their work installed at a Disney location.*

*ImagiNations opens up the opportunity for students to showcase their skills and talents to Imagineering through a Disney-related project. Provided with a project challenge, students and recent graduates work in teams to deliver a concept in a similar way to how Imagineers develop their blue-sky projects. In a matter of weeks, teams have to leverage their various artistic, technical, and communication skills to prepare a submission that will appeal to judges whose backgrounds include a wide array of creative and technical disciplines.*

ImagiNations was created to expand opportunities to attract new Imagineers by reaching out to a diversified population. In doing so, we made it clear that we wanted the Imagineering staff to reflect the society we live in—and the guests who come to our parks and resorts, not just in

America, but also around the world. And perhaps most importantly: it's a *team* competition, reflecting the collaborative way Imagineering's 140 different disciplines work together on a single project. As a result, entries in our annual competition have come from teams at one school or association, or two or more individuals working together on a single project despite being located hundreds or thousands of miles apart.

Here is what some Imagineers have said about their experience:

> *"In 2005, I entered the ImagiNations program at Walt Disney Imagineering, a competition designed to find new diverse talent from around the world. At the time, I knew very little about Imagineering. What I did know came from a few short segments on the Disney Channel that I saw as a kid called 'Imagineer That!' I was in awe of what the Imagineers did, but I never considered it as something I could realistically do for a career. Nevertheless, I entered the competition and gave it my all. I was studying illustration at California State University, Fullerton, and I thought I was destined for a career as a comic book artist. If there's one thing I've learned at Imagineering, it's that you never know what the future might hold. Even the best laid out plans will inevitably change.*
>
> *"Shortly after competing, I was awarded an internship working at the Imagineering Resource Center, or the IRC, as we call it. During my internship, I was able to get to know some of the most talented and creative people working in themed*

entertainment. And not just get to know them, but show them what I could do, too!"

**Brian Crosby,** Creative Designer
(His Cal State Fullerton project was based on the Disney film *The Rocketeer*.)

"During my senior year in college (University of Hawai`i at Mānoa—1993), I discovered how to turn my dream of having a creative job into a reality. A friend of mine needed a fine arts major to help with an 'ImagiNations' competition he was working on, so I naturally volunteered. We designed an E-ticket thrill attraction based on an original story featuring the friendship between three legendary cryptozoological creatures (characters). Through this process I not only made new friends as we built a team to take on the challenges of the project, but I also made connections with intriguing people at Walt Disney Imagineering. Bob Hope once said, 'I've always been in the right place at the right time. Of course, I've steered myself there.' Yes, we were lucky to be chosen out of the many participating teams to land a coveted internship (straight out of college), but we were also incredibly driven by our passions for the project and worked hard to make sure it was the best representation of our talents."

**Owen Yoshino,** Creative Director, Principal Concept Designer, Tokyo Disneyland Projects

(Note: Two other Imagineers whose advice appears on these pages came to Imagineering through the ImagiNations program. They are **Daniel Joseph** and **Dex Tanksley**.)

WEAR YOUR GUESTS SHOES • PASSION • 3 ORGANIZ
TY • 9 FOR EVERY OUNCE OF TREATMENT, PRE
TION—NEVER STOP LEARNING • 7 TELL
UAL MAGNET) • COLLABORA
KNOW YOUR AUDIE
TAKE A CH

# WE GET LETTERS . . .

**. . . and we answer them!**

"One of the things I do in my 'spare time,'" says creative designer David Fisher, "is answer letters from kids who dream of one day becoming Imagineers. I'm not sure why Marty chose me to do this (way back in the nineties) . . . but I was honored to take on the task."

On the following page is an example of a letter Dave wrote to a young fan in February 2014:

**Walt Disney Imagineering**

Dear Kylie:

Thanks for writing us here at Walt Disney Imagineering and sorry it's taken so long for us to reply. As you already seem to know, we are the creative design and development division of Walt Disney Parks and Resorts responsible for the creation of all Disney resorts, theme parks and attractions, cruise ships and new entertainment venues.

It's always nice to hear from people such as you who are fascinated by both the Disney parks and Walt Disney Imagineering, and express an interest in perhaps one day becoming an Imagineer. Just like you, I wanted to work for Disney when I was young (I was 13). I sent my letter to Disneyland, asking how to get a job. (Though I'm guessing the letter had nothing to do with it, I eventually got one, working at the park in the Custodial Department while I attended the University of Southern California, majoring in journalism and English. After graduation, I worked my way into my current position here at Imagineering.)

Based in Glendale, California (with Imagineers in Florida, Hawaii, Paris, Tokyo, Hong Kong and Shanghai—the places where we have Disney parks and resorts), our team includes nearly 1,700 show designers, architects, engineers, model designers, writers, technicians and other talents (more than 140 disciplines in all). One thing we have in common is that we're storytellers. Our goal is to create memorable stories and experiences and we do this through our lands, rides, attractions, shops, restaurants and resorts.

Another thing we have in common is that we like to make people happy. This may sound kind of corny, but perhaps the best thing about being an Imagineer is being able to create parks, attractions and shows that entertain people. One of the proudest moments for any Imagineer comes when an attraction is finished and he or she sees people (we call them guests) leave with smiles on their faces, excited at what they've just seen or experienced.

Your letter ended up on my desk, which is a good thing, since I know a thing or two about Imagineers and becoming an Imagineer.

From a purely legal standpoint, you must be at least 18 years of age to work full-time at Imagineering, but most Imagineers are often graduates of top universities and professional schools around the world who have developed their talents and honed their skills with years of experience either here or with other companies.

© Disney

If you think you'd maybe one day like to be an Imagineer, I can offer the following advice:

1. Try not to limit your interest to the world of Disney. Let it be a point of entry to the discovery of other subjects, such as cultural studies, robotics, film disciplines, art, history, whatever. Knowledge of Disney does not guarantee a job with Disney, nor is it a requirement for one.
2. Pursue a career or a subject that you truly enjoy. The important thing is not what you do but that you love what you do. There is no major at any college, nor is there any profession, known as Imagineering. Imagineers are first and foremost "something else," such as an architect, an engineer or a financial analyst. It's that expertise and talent in something else that landed them at Imagineering. I'm a writer and it's my love of, talent for and skill at writing that landed me a job here at Imagineering. That, and a bit of luck (which is always important, as any Imagineer will tell you).

Because of the number and diversity of disciplines we have here at Imagineering, it's hard to suggest courses of study or even specific courses in high school and college that would best prepare someone to become an Imagineer. However, when you start thinking about college (it will be here before you know it!), you should know that different universities offer different experiences for each individual. Because of this, I recommend that you find a college or university that you are comfortable with and that will offer you the kinds of programs and activities that are right for you. After all, it's not the college that's important to us—it's the person.

We do offer internships to qualified college students and recent college graduates on a limited basis. You can check out the offering at www.disneyinterns.com (we can be found under the Walt Disney Parks and Resorts tab). You can also learn about ImagiNations, an annual design competition sponsored by Walt Disney Imagineering, at www.disneyimaginations.com.

In the end, all I can say, Kylie, is keep following your dreams, and who knows? Maybe one day you will get the chance to become an Imagineer.

Warm regards and best wishes,

David Fisher / Story Development

1401 Flower St., Glendale, CA 91201

© Disney

Now let's imagine that you have written a letter to an Imagineer whose job description or background especially interests you. On the following pages, you will meet some of the best and the brightest, learn what they believe is important to their careers, and even hear a few words about their favorite projects.

* * * * * * * * * *

**Alfredo Ayala** has just completed his twentieth year at Imagineering. Born in Los Angeles, he majored in engineering and chemistry at Cal State Los Angeles. He's a principal creative lead in Research and Development, he holds over ten patents, and his favorite project is his *next* project. "I truly love starting out with a blank sheet of paper; this is where creativity lives!"

*I have been at Imagineering for over twenty years. Being an Imagineer has allowed me to work with the best creative folks the world has to offer. Many people ask me what I do as an Imagineer and how does someone become an Imagineer? The simple answer is that I help immerse people in real, physical three-dimensional experiences where the magic of Disney stories comes to life.*

*Here is a list of the things that you must achieve to do my job:*

*1. You must be willing to never stop learning.*
*2. You must not only practice your art or science, but also push yourself to discover new secrets.*
*3. You cannot be afraid of failing.*
*4. You must love working with large, diverse teams and share ideas.*

5. You cannot have preconceptions. To be a great artist, you must have great observation skills; to be a great scientist, you must have great observation skills. Science and art are fundamentally the same in spirit.
6. You must be willing to respect yourself and those around you.
7. You must always evolve how to go from an idea to reality.
8. You must learn to have thick skin. If you are willing to have your ideas criticized, then you will make a good Imagineer.
9. If you find potential and opportunity where others see obstacles, then you are an Imagineer.
10. Don't fear change, embrace it!

Well, these are my two cents on being an Imagineer. The way you gain these skills is through education. Find your passion, and when you do, don't let go. I guarantee, it will be a fun trip.

\* \* \* \* \* \* \* \* \* \*

**Yves Benyeta,** executive creative director, is back in Glendale after a two-year assignment at the Tokyo Disney Resort. Born in Toulon, France, he began his Disney career twenty-four years ago at Disneyland Paris—still his favorite project.

Dear young designer,
Be confident in yourself as a designer. Be funny, serious, self-promotional, irreverent, whatever—just be yourself. Instinct and intuition are powerful. Learn to trust them, but remember that the Golden Rule actually works. Some of your best design decisions will ultimately be saying no to a person or to a project.

*Be authentic. The most powerful asset you have is your individuality, what makes you unique. Don't work in a particular style. Rather, develop a personal approach to your creative work. Study the work of others to understand it, not to duplicate it.*

*Find and save relevant and interesting things and pass them along to your friends and coworkers. Share your experience with others; it's a nice way to recycle your thoughts and get more points of view. Seek criticism, not praise.*

*Work harder than anyone else and you will always benefit from the effort. Never give up, but don't expect it to be easy. Do your homework.*

*Get off the computer and connect with real people and culture. Make things with your hands. Innovation in thinking is not enough. Take a break from your comfort zone and experiment with an approach you've never tried before. Don't be above anything. Sometimes the small jobs can lead to big ones. It is an important thing to love the whole design process, from the beginning to the end.*

*Never nod your head and say you got it when you don't. Say, "I don't understand what you mean." It's not rude. They won't think you are stupid. Never accept a terrible or wrong answer.*

*Don't forget to have fun! Otherwise how can you expect our Guests to have fun with those experiences you are creating?*

* * * * * * * * * *

**Fintan Burke,** technical director/principal animation, is a native of Limerick City, Ireland. He left school at age sixteen but attended night school in Limerick and took French language study courses at Westminster College in London and a leadership course at UCLA. His favorite project was Disney's Animal Kingdom, "because it challenged me like nothing before."

*What made me the Imagineer I am today is the teaching my father gave me as I apprenticed in his garage as a "Panel Beater." My father took me out of school at the age of sixteen. He took me into the garage, Paul Burke and Co. Panel Beaters, and this is where I completed my five-year apprentice program to become a panel beater, known in America as a "body man" in the automotive repair business.*

*I hated my father for taking me out of school, but I didn't realize what a gift he was giving me. I became strong, in character, in my skills . . . shaping metal, welding, repairing, and painting. I could fix anything and make anything. It also inspired me to leave home and go back to school. I worked in London (at a Rolls-Royce repair shop). I worked in LA (Vel's Parnelli Jones Body Shop and its racing division) and also had a small shop with my good friend Charlie Eddy, where we restored old European classics and worked on concept cars for Mitsubishi and Honda. I was also fortunate to work in the racing world with the Can-Am series and Indy Bullet for Al Unser Jr.*

*This all paved the way for my Disney career. Disney has many roads one can travel; you just have to believe in yourself and never let anyone tell you, "You can't do that." In fact, that's when the* fun *begins.*

\* \* \* \* \* \* \* \* \* \*

**Oscar Cobos Jr.** is a designer, principal in the architecture design studio, who's celebrating twenty-six years at Imagineering. Born in Camargo, Chihuahua, Mexico, Cobos earned his architecture degree at the University of Southern California. His favorite project was the Arabian Coast area of Tokyo DisneySea, because "I had the opportunity to design the architectural environment of the whole land."

*How did I end up becoming an Imagineer? First of all, it was not my goal to become an Imagineer when I was searching within myself what I ought to become, what I ought to study during that critical high school senior time in my life. Many young people at that age find themselves having to make choices that will impact and shape the rest of their lives. At that moment in our lives, we have to ask ourselves, "What do I really enjoy doing?" or "In what area am I really gifted?" Being true to that and to yourself is the beginning of being the best that you can be in any one thing. So first, you need to dig deep in your heart and mind to head into that true-to-yourself direction in life.*

*After working with several architecture firms in my early career years, the firm for which I worked was consulted to do architectural drawings for what was then called EPCOT Center. All of a sudden my thoughts went to that day when I visited the House of the Future!*

*I was practicing what I loved for the Disney Company that had inspired me to choose my path in architecture. My career path was not to work for a certain company, but to develop myself in a field in which I used my gifts, my talents, my passion, my love; then where and when I could apply that was wide open. Fortunately Walt Disney Imagineering could use someone with my skills, where I could apply those things I learned and loved in a very passionate way, designing and building those wonderful Disney parks that people all over the world enjoy and are inspired by.*

*Now I think, "If I had shaped my career to work for Imagineering, would my life be a disappointment if I was never hired by Disney?" But no, I shaped my career by things that I love, that I feel I have been given natural gifts for, and that has not brought me to disappointment; it has brought me to a fulfilling life and a fulfilling career, practicing what I love and enjoy and at the same time creating some unforgettable environments and experiences for my fellow citizens to be inspired by in turn.*

*Be true to yourself.*

\* \* \* \* \* \* \* \* \* \*

**Tim Delaney** now leads his own company, Tim J. Delaney Design, after a thirty-four-year Imagineering career. Born just down the street from Imagineering's Glendale headquarters, he graduated from Art Center College of Design in Pasadena, California. His favorite project: "Leading the team in creating Discoveryland, a new version of Tomorrowland at Disneyland Paris."

## TEN THINGS IT TOOK ME THIRTY-FOUR YEARS TO LEARN AND APPRECIATE AT IMAGINEERING

1. *BE CURIOUS/SEEK KNOWLEDGE: In the spirit of Herbie Ryman and John Hench, learning and discovery are lifelong adventures. In my last five years at WDI, my office was just ten feet from John Hench's, and every afternoon I saw the books and magazines arrive from the library that were to be John's nightly reading material. The diversity of subjects and variety of materials were astounding! As for Herbie, he taught me the value of the sketchbook and the recording of ideas and images to fulfill one's internal knowledge. The understanding of your creative self forges the personal and emotional power that all projects must have.*

2. *CREATIVITY COMES IN MANY FORMS: All successful enterprises are based on creativity. For me, creativity is the process of looking at all problems and projects and finding the most unique solution. Creativity is not just for the arts. At WDI the best estimators are the ones who help use the estimates in creative ways to move a project forward.*

3. *HAVE COURAGE: Believe in your ideas. If your ideas are based on inspiration, research, and a sincere desire to create something new and special, then stand strong regardless of the opposition. I was called to Frank Wells's office one afternoon, where, with finger pounding my chest, he said, "It is your job, as Imagineers, to tell us, Michael (Eisner) and me, what is new and the right thing to do; it is our job to decide if you are right!" Although this was great advice from a great man, it rarely made my life easier with project management.*

4. *TALENT: Every person has it. The key is to find how one's*

talent is used in the most effective way. Think of a project team as a high-performance automobile where every part must work in harmony to move it forward.

5. **BE A TEAM PLAYER:** No project is built by one person. Believe in the team; they are your project family. Every team is made up of different talents; using them effectively is the key to success.

6. **BE A TEAM LEADER:** No team moves forward without leadership, and powerful leadership moves it faster and further than anyone can imagine. Remember, there are many managers in the world but far too few leaders.

7. **PASSION:** As they say, nothing worthwhile gets done without it.

8. **BE A POSITIVE FORCE:** The world is filled with negative energy, but nothing is successful without an uncompromising positive force behind it.

9. **RESPECT THE BUDGET:** All successful creative enterprises must live in the real world, and respecting the project budget and the project schedule are key to success.

10. **IF THE PROCESS ISN'T FUN, THEN THE PRODUCT WON'T BE:** The world is getting lost in too much process and too many meetings. Learn to have fun.

\* \* \* \* \* \* \* \* \* \*

**David Durham** currently wears two hats: he's the Creative Designers Studio lead, and he heads the Inspirational Blue Sky Program. Born in Salt Lake City, he graduated from California Institute of Technology (Caltech) and, after several years at Disneyland, has been an Imagineer for twenty-four years. His favorite project: the Cosmic Waves Fountain in Tomorrowland at Disneyland. "It allowed guests the pure fun of simply playing in water—the kind of fun we used to have on the playground while growing up . . . but often forget as we get older."

*There are so many lessons that I've learned through the years that I would have loved to pass down to a younger me. . . .The problem is . . . I wouldn't have believed my older self. The me of today and the me of twenty-five years ago (when I first started at Imagineering) are two very different people. Life and life's lessons have crafted the me that stands here today. Nuggets of wisdom would simply bounce off my head if thrown at my younger doppelganger.*

*I could tell myself, "Readjust your expectations, because everything takes longer than you think it will." But I'm not sure it would really sink in. There are many Imagineers, like myself, who had to wait years to get in. In real estate it's "location, location, location"; in entertainment it's "timing, timing, timing." It doesn't matter if you're the best in the world at a given task; if the company you want to work for isn't hiring, then that particular door is temporarily closed. Are you patient? Will you be persistent?*

*I would tell my younger self that it's important to know what you want to do in life. Artist, engineer, estimator, architect, producer, model maker . . . ? The list goes on and on. Over 140 disciplines, which ONE are you? Imagineering won't teach you a trade. If you're being hired as an estimator, then you should already know how to be an estimator. Imagineering will teach you the ins and outs of the unique culture and specifics of the process. Remember that you are being hired in your area of expertise; you don't get to try a little of this and a little of that and then see if something over there interests you instead. You need to make a choice at the outset. So what do you want to be when you grow up? Choose your area of interest and that will affect what classes you take in school, what extracurricular activities you become involved in, what hobbies you choose. . . . And they should all be something you enjoy and are passionate about. If you aren't passionate about the specific work you do, then you're in the wrong field. Passion isn't a requirement for a job, but it's often what separates the great ones from everyone else.*

*And lastly I would tell my younger self, "Be careful what you wish for." . . . Imagineering is an amazing place, full of fantastic people creating wondrous attractions. We work unbelievably hard, quietly in the background so that everything seems effortless. But Imagineers are some of the hardest-working professionals in the world. If you don't have a strong and determined work ethic that values hard work, teamwork, attention to detail, long hours, international travel, creative tension, and constantly pushing yourself . . . then maybe Imagineering isn't for you. But if . . . if you have a passion for creating new worlds, if you believe anything is possible, if you believe—as the Imagineering mission statement says—that "Happy People Make the World a Better Place," then maybe, just maybe, the timing will be right, the years of preparation will come to fruition, and your unique skills will be able to find a place at Walt Disney Imagineering.*

\* \* \* \* \* \* \* \* \* \*

**Elisabeth (Eli) Erlandson** earned an architecture degree from the University of Southern California (USC) and retired as a principal architect in 2014. Her native country (she was born in São Paulo, Brazil) has had a lasting influence on her career.

*My dream since childhood was to work at Disney someday. As I developed, my passions became very evident to me. I was an artist since the age of three, and I wanted to also become an architect since the age of eleven. I have earnestly pursued both interests since then.*

*In 1975, my father gave me an unusual gift, which changed my life. On the day of my graduation from USC, he handed me a blank application to WED Enterprises. He knew my dream, and he was helping me get it. WED was a place I had never heard of before. At that time, it was a secret place, hidden in an unassuming commercial warehouse neighborhood of Glendale, California, with no signs declaring its existence. I dared to apply that same week and was happy that it led to my long career at WED/WDI.*

*To young, inexperienced individuals, the best way to prepare yourself for WDI is to know what field you are interested in, study it well, excel above the norm, believe in yourself, and be bold and dare yourself* to apply to work at WDI. Once inside, put your ego in perspective and be humbled by the outstanding talent and immense realm of experienced individuals from all disciplines that surround you. Be humbled enough to understand that you have a lot to learn from them, but don't be so humbled that it freezes you into a "fear of failure" mode.

Another aspect that makes a person a good Imagineer is their having pursued other interests beyond their chosen profession. At WDI, in architecture, there have been individuals who pursued music, writing, performance arts, photography, painting, dance, sculpture, costume design, woodwork, poetry, and various sports. One unusual case comes to mind: Stan Jukowicz was an outstanding artist in the craft of architectural thematic design who worked at WED in the 1970s and into the 1980s. He loved bugs—he possessed a world-renowned collection of various species, and he also had a personal farm of silkworms under his desk at WED, which he brought up as his own children. He fed them daily with leaves from the mulberry tree in our company's cafeteria patio and assured the temperature was always correct under his desk for his silkworms to become beautiful butterflies.

I believe that these other interests that one is passionate about are crucial. These make it possible for us to work for many years on very difficult projects, with little breathers in between. It is where we find peace and strength to continue. Because of these outside interests, we also gain a deeper understanding of each other and get along better when the going is tough.

Our projects are difficult; even the simple things are not simple in how we do things. Working at WDI is not for anyone looking for an easy ride to success in their field. You may be smart, but so is everyone around you. It is for those who love difficult challenges and difficult situations. It is for those who navigate forward with a common team goal in mind. Not everyone is suited for this, but those who are find it quite fulfilling.

Learning, understanding, and utilizing Mickey's Ten Commandments is also quite helpful. Beyond these, it is also important to have a great attitude, a sense of humor, and a character that can gain respect.

Another useful skill one must develop is presenting oneself verbally in front of an audience to clearly explain an idea and how it fits the "story" that the team is creating. Understanding the importance of "story," and for which audience it is being created, is crucial—it is at the heart of what we do.

In architecture, it is also important to know art and architectural history and corresponding details. The details are what tell the story of the environments we create. WDI architects never stop researching and learning; that is how we feed our minds with inspirational imagery.

Not everyone is suited for this Imagineering endurance run. Those who are suited for it create and participate in a most formidable and ultimately fun ride of a lifetime!

* * * * * * * * * *

**Peggie Fariss** was born in Fresno, California, graduated with a B.A. degree in English from Cal State Fullerton, and has taken "lots and lots of UCLA Extension classes." Beginning her Disney career at Disneyland, Peggie has been an Imagineer for thirty-eight years, many of them working with corporate sponsors in the parks. She is just completing five years as the creative leader of the Imagineering team at Disneyland Paris. Her favorite projects are a potpourri of new developments, with a special fondness for Epcot projects, including her "deep dive" into history for the story in Spaceship Earth, and her organization of EPCOT Conferences, including the establishment of the Pavilion Advisory Boards.

> *"I don't know . . . but I'll find out."*
> *I first heard these words, nearly fifty years ago, when I was a young Disneyland cast member, working on Storybook Land Canal Boats, attending a Disney University orientation program. The session was preparation for what we might expect when we were onstage and what would be expected of us. This particular message told us two things: First, nobody expected you to have all the answers, so relax and be honest ("I don't know . . ."). The second part of the message demanded action (". . . I'll find out."). Your job wasn't done until you'd found and conveyed the requested information.*
> *Later, I discovered that this dictum was one of Marty Sklar's "cardinal rules" for Imagineering and*

no doubt had found its way into the Disneyland training curriculum because of him. In any event, it had become my mantra and has enriched my life in myriad ways because it gave me permission—in fact, commanded me—to explore. . . .

In my early Disney days, the questions were pretty simple: "What time is the parade?" "Where are the nearest restrooms?" "What are the names of the Seven Dwarfs?" So providing the right answers was pretty easy. "Five o'clock." "Just beyond King Arthur Carrousel." "Happy, Sleepy, Sneezy, Dopey, Doc, Grumpy, and Bashful."

During my spell as a meeting planner at Walt Disney World, the questions required consulting experts: "What wine would pair well with prime rib?" "What logistical considerations would be involved in moving a thousand people from location X to location Y so they'd have a good view of the fireworks—and what about a rain plan?"

A few years later, during the development of Epcot, the questions became even more interesting and served as gateways to a world of fascinating topics and remarkable people: "Who in the world was doing groundbreaking work in agriculture, in oceanic research, in space?" "What were the key technological achievements in communications over the past forty thousand years?" "What did the Phoenician language sound like?" "What instruments should our Renaissance musicians be playing, and who plays those instruments today?"

What I've discovered in all of this is that learning

*opens you up to the world and to new possibilities. It keeps your perspectives fresh and your imagination flexible. So be brave and resourceful, nurture your sense of wonder, celebrate your curiosity, and embrace the delicious adventures awaiting you as you tackle the unknown. "Go. . . . Find out!"*

\* \* \* \* \* \* \* \* \* \*

**Joe Herrington,** principal audio media designer, was born in Houston, Texas, and after attending Odessa College and San Diego State University, he thought he was destined to teach astronomy. But his love for technology led him into radio and television, then into film and sound production. A thirty-four-year Imagineer, Herrington loved "breaking new technological ground" with the Radiator Springs Racers in Disney California Adventure and the Indiana Jones vehicle in Disneyland.

*I see many young people who show up wanting positions in my field. Some are interns and some are not, but in almost every case, they are bright, skilled, and energetic. There is no lack of passion. They have the credentials, but there is often a missing ingredient: frequently they lack the kind of foundation needed to properly build a future here. So what do they need to know most?*

*These young candidates fall into two categories. One category strains the gears and never really finds a good fit, while the other seems to fit naturally into a niche that syncs harmoniously into the fabric of our unique, creative environment.*

The first are the young graduates who show up at our door believing that they are the shining gem that we can't do without. They have been raised by mentors who told them they were wonderful while shielding them from the reality of hard work, consequences, and failure. They come to us in a bubble, oblivious to what they don't know but so very anxious to show and tell what they do know.

The second group somehow missed that deceptive, glittering mud puddle. They had mentors who showed them that stumbling was just part of life, but learning how to get up, again and again, was the trait that made the difference in that life's success. Those mentors showed them how to lay their life foundation with the bricks and steel of humility, hard work, and ethical behavior. First and foremost, they learned their place and responsibility in society and then they learned how to build their skills on that foundation.

The resulting attitude inherent within these two groups determines whether they show up here in a glass bubble believing they are jewels of colossal brilliance or wearing a cloak of humility, recognizing they have come to collaborate with the most creative minds in the world.

The first group believes they have their education. The second understands that real learning is just beginning and they strive to become sponges, sucking up everything they possibly can. Their humble attitude is . . . I came to learn. Please teach me everything you can.

*So you want a career as an Imagineer? Let time-tested values govern the way you let mentors have access to your intellect. Be patient, yet anxious to listen to trusted mentors. Recognize that stumbling is a learning process. Learning from it and getting up over and over is the path to success. Know that all the knowledge you gain in school is not wisdom but must be applied with humility, patience, and integrity.*

*We have no shortage of young people coming to us with high skill sets. But to preserve the uniqueness of the Disney brand while growing it to meet the demands of the future, those skill sets should simply be seen as prerequisites to learn from the masters. Attitude is everything. It can shroud great skill and creative genius or let it soar.*

\* \* \* \* \* \* \* \* \* \*

**Zsolt Hormay** puts aside his interest in music (he plays flute, classical and acoustic guitar, and Renaissance lute) and sports (he spent two years as a member of the Hungarian national hockey team) to focus on placemaking and production design at Imagineering. Born in Pécs, Hungary, he studied practical and fine art in Budapest. Now a creative vice president after thirteen years at Imagineering, Zsolt says the Tree of Life at Disney's Animal Kingdom is his favorite project because he had, in his words, "the opportunity to bring together a top-notch international team of sculptors to curate nearly three hundred detailed animal carvings in the 145-foot-tall tree"— a sculptural statement of the endless beauty and intercon-nected nature of the earth's many creatures.

*You want to be an Imagineer? Do you want to make magic? Magic does not come easy; magic can only become magic when you have given everything you've got and more to make the impossible a reality. Imagineers are always striving for new opportunities to advance what we do to stay on the cutting edge. Imagineers are always working to understand and utilize the most modern technology to stay ahead of the game and yet be cognizant of the history of where we came from, the vision of Walt Disney himself, and where we are headed into the future. To be the best and nothing but the best!*

*I strongly believe that working for Walt Disney Imagineering is the ultimate satisfaction for any young creative mind that is committed to follow their dreams. Once in the door, you will find a world that you will never want to leave. I have been, I am, and I always will be the proudest Imagineer.*

\* \* \* \* \* \* \* \* \* \*

Creative development executive **Shelby Jiggets-Tivony** came to Disney in 2001 to develop theatrical shows for the parks and Disney Cruise Line. A native of Richmond, Virginia, she attended Virginia Commonwealth University. Aulani, the Disney resort and spa in Hawaii, challenged Shelby and the team "to put culture first and—drawing upon the knowledge of a community of native artists and speakers—to create a resort designed with the aesthetic of a 'little d' (for Disney) and 'big h' (for Hawaii)."

*Growing up in Richmond, Virginia, in the 1970s,
I was a beneficiary of what would become the
last vestiges of Lyndon Johnson's "Great Society
Programs." Tickets to performances of Mozart's* The
Magic Flute *and Prokofiev's* Peter and the Wolf, *as
well as a screening of Franco Zeffirelli's* Romeo and
Juliet, *were all government subsidized. The National
Endowment for the Humanities sent local artists to
our public schools. My all-black elementary school
on the north side of Richmond had a musician come
to teach our class how to play the dulcimer . . . the
dulcimer! Why on earth would a bunch of city kids
need to know how to play a stringed instrument used
to make folk music in the Appalachian Mountains?
What I didn't know at the time was that even as I
rolled my eyes while we played "Oh Shenandoah"
and made fun of Olivia Hussey's accent (Google her), I
was falling in love with the performing arts. A touring
company of Alvin Ailey American Dance Theater at
Richmond's Carpenter Theatre Center sealed the
deal. The beautiful Judith Jamison (Google her)
performed a piece called* Cry. *I'd never seen anything
like it—a statuesque African American woman
dressed in white, dancing her way through grief and
triumph. It changed me forever.*

*In college I only managed to succeed in getting
good grades in classes that let me read great stuff
and write about it. A recently unearthed transcript
verified this fact: Fiction into Film—A; Biology—F.
After college my mother presented me with the civil
service test for the city of Richmond. If I had known*

*about muscle testing then, I'm sure a simple pressing down on the hand that was holding the application would have shown no strength whatsoever. Having no idea how my interests and talents could lead to any kind of meaningful profession, I chose, instead, to move through my future exploring things that I enjoyed. I liked food and people, which led me to a series of jobs in local restaurants. My love of books led me to work in a bookstore, a library and, eventually, a card/stationery store. Finally, attending a job fair for administrative theater jobs in New Jersey landed me gigs writing grants for the McCarter Theatre in Princeton, New Jersey, and working in the box office of the Crossroads Theatre in New Brunswick—a ten-minute train ride away. Over time, my ability to read and analyze text landed me an opportunity as an unpaid script reader for Crossroads and then the offer to be their literary associate and eventually the literary manager. That led to becoming the associate dramaturge at Lincoln Center Theater and my move to New York City, followed by the coveted position of director of play development of the Joseph Papp Public Theater.*

*Now I'm at Walt Disney Imagineering, and after more than a decade of creating shows in our parks and resorts, I transitioned to a role where I support the work of the gifted designers who create our attractions and lands around the world. Many of their names you may never know, because their work proudly goes under one name: Walt Disney.*

*Here's what I know I know:*

- Exposure to the performing and visual arts makes us well-rounded and better-informed people.
- Don't do anything that makes you feel sad or unenthusiastic, or that your gut tells you is a bad idea.
- Keep moving forward; when one door closes, go find a window to climb through.
- Don't let your mom decide your future—Mother doesn't always know best.
- Adopt a philosophy for living. Use something as a guidepost; you'll need it during the tough times. I try to follow Miguel Angel Ruiz's The Four Agreements:

1. Be Impeccable with Your Word
2. Don't Take Anything Personally
3. Don't Make Assumptions
4. Always Do Your Best

\* \* \* \* \* \* \* \* \* \*

**Daniel Joseph** is a senior special effects and illusion designer—an Imagineer for seven years since winning first place in the 2006 ImagiNations competition. Born in Wilmington, Delaware, Joseph is a graduate of the University of the Arts in Philadelphia. His favorite project is the GM Test Track "because I got to work in a park I care immensely about (Epcot) and with a team of wonderful people who are now my lifelong friends."

*Working as a special effects and illusion designer*
*at Walt Disney Imagineering has given me a certain*
*perspective on life and what I see every day that*
*I think is very different from any of my friends or*

family. I grew up seeing things very differently from everyone around me: my brother, my best friend, even my parents. I thought this was a disability; where I saw a bunch of squiggly lines and cryptic text, my schoolmates saw grammar tests and reading assignments. I soon found out that I had what was called "learning disabilities." This must have been why I couldn't read as well or as fast as everyone else around me! I felt very inferior, and reading aloud in class was equivalent to a gigantic child-eating monster. I found myself needing an outlet for this energy and frustration, so I started taking things apart and making new things from them. I would take everything in sight apart. A remote control for an old TV would become a blinking light beacon for a miniature Sky Lift. The motor for moving the car up and down a string would of course come from a polishing rock tumbler. A fan motor with an old funnel and some stripped copper wire would become a sparking light! This went on and on.

I started bringing these contraptions and inventions to school for show-and-tell. I soon noticed a very familiar face that my friends and teachers would make when I would show them and describe to them how these things worked. They would explain how amazing these things were but also how they really didn't quite understand how I made them or how they worked. I realized the faces they were making were out of perplexity and embarrassment. I then connected the dots: this was the same feeling (and face) I had when I would try to work through *grammar and reading assignments. It then hit me: there were more of them who didn't understand my contraptions and inventions than the only one of me that didn't understand the grammar and reading lessons. Did this mean I was weird? Or did this mean something else?*

*After showing more and more friends and family my creations, I realized I had people coming to me with questions about how to do something, or how something worked. This is where I realized my learning "disability" was more of a learning "difference" and also something that was a rare thing that people were interested in! I learned with hard work I could learn grammar, reading, and even math like everyone else. I also learned I had something in me that other people didn't naturally have. This was something to cherish and nourish: the gift of unending curiosity, which always leads to one thing—creation.*

\* \* \* \* \* \* \* \* \* \*

**Michael Jung,** vice president of theatrical development for WDI Creative Entertainment, was born in Detroit, Michigan, and received his BFA in art history and theater from Macalester College and an MFA in theater directing from CalArts. His fourteen years at Imagineering have included "so many amazing projects—but some of my favorites have been creating original musicals for *Finding Nemo*, *Aladdin*, and *The Lion King*" for the parks.

*Nearly eight years ago, I had the honor of being invited by Marty Sklar to participate on a panel of*

CalArts alumni who were working at WDI. I was surprised that this panel was the first step in establishing a deeper relationship between Imagineering and CalArts, especially given that CalArts was founded in the image of WED Enterprises, Walt's famed think tank of creative artists and designers. From that moment on, I was smitten with the idea of fostering a deeper connectivity between the Institute and Imagineering. I was especially inspired by the work that Imagineer Bruce Vaughn was doing with UCLA, where he taught a seminar and suggested that WDI consider a similar program with CalArts. We began by inviting the faculty to tour our facilities and meet with some of our creative leadership. We were reminded of Walt's original words in describing his vision of CalArts: "What young artists need is a school where they can learn a variety of skills, a place where there is cross-pollination."

This exciting legacy served as a foundation for the future. An annual WDI Day at CalArts was established where Imagineers from a diverse array of disciplines share their experiences and journey to WDI. We also began a core curriculum in Themed and Immersive Experience and Design classes featuring a talented array of luminaries and instructors.

Perhaps not surprisingly, the act of teaching has not only been a wonderful opportunity to share lessons learned but has been in itself a true master class. When students ask me for advice as they begin their professional careers, I am reminded of my own journey and once more the words of Walt Disney: "If you keep busy, your work might lead you into paths *you might not expect. I've always . . . gone on quests not knowing where they would lead."*

Stay open to new experiences and take the path that will offer the most challenge and opportunity for growth.

* * * * * * * * * *

Born in La Union, a province north of Manila, the capital of the Philippines, **Abe Quibin** studied at the University of Santo Tomas, built by the Spaniards in 1611. Now director of concept architecture and relocated in Shanghai, he has been an Imagineer for forty-one years. He considers Tokyo DisneySea his favorite project because "I was fortunate to contribute to all three zones in the park and also lucky enough to work with the Japanese builders."

*Few people are lucky enough to realize their dreams. I felt so fortunate when WED hired me in Florida in 1973. At that time I thought, How can a young man from the Philippines be given a chance to work for the world-famous entertainment company named Disney? All I can say is, what a joyride it has been to be involved in the design of eight theme parks and resorts around the world with the most brilliant minds in the industry. It was so much fun that I did not realize forty-plus years had passed.*

*Over the years, through the internship program in WDI, I had the privilege of helping architecture students from different universities in the country learn theme park and resort design. We are guided by Marty's Ten Commandments, aka Mickey's Ten Commandments. Some of them came back after their graduation and became project architects, designers, and executives within Disney. Most of them became successful because of their dedication, hard work, and creative accomplishments. The best reward is when you see something you created on paper come to fruition, especially when you are at the site helping to build it.*

*Currently I am in China working on my fourth foreign assignment, Shanghai Disney Resort's Treasure Cove. With me on this project are young and bright architects who will continue Disney's tradition in the future. I can see their great enthusiasm and drive to make this project a success, just like in the past. Everyone seems to be equal to the task and the challenges that come with the new language and culture.*

*I am forever thankful for the chance and trust given to me by WDI and will treasure the friendships with all my colleagues in this great company.*

\* \* \* \* \* \* \* \* \* \*

A true New Yorker among Imagineers, **Lanny Smoot** was born in Brooklyn and attended Columbia University in the city, where he received his bachelor of science in electrical engineering in 1977 and his master of science in electrical engineering in 1998. Now in his sixteenth year at Imagineering, Lanny is a Disney Research Fellow—the highest level of technical achievement in the Disney Research hierarchy. His favorite project was "levitating Leota," making the head of Madam Leota "escape" her confines and "fly" around the Séance Room in the Haunted Mansion.

### Growing Up

*A young person growing up with a strong interest in science (or any other "specialized" field) often feels as though there is no one else in the world that likes what they like, or does what they do. Without an Internet, and when the Encyclopedia Britannica (if you could afford one) is the last word in "instant information access," things take a little longer! On the other hand, the lack of easy answers can encourage a craving for knowledge and hands-on experimentation.*

*In the case of budding electronics engineers, we are the ones picking up old radios and televisions (to mold them into new gadgets). We are the ones whose bedrooms look more like a vintage television repair shop than a place to sleep. We spend time in the local library trying to satisfy our craving to know more about our interests. In school we constantly raise our hands to answer science questions (when other kids are more interested in games or sports). As we grow older, we begin to wonder whether we will ever meet people who do what we do and like what we like. We're not even aware that one could possibly make a living doing something that just seems like so much fun!*

### Early Schooling

*Again, I was always interested in science. I wandered for a while into physics, then took a brief detour into chemistry, started by a family friend giving me a chemistry set; however, I found chemistry to be a bit limiting (and messy!).*

*I was interested in microscopy, again, after*

receiving a gift of a kit microscope, and astronomy (I traded an old bicycle for an even older telescope). It was through that telescope, probably at the age of twelve or thirteen, that I first saw the rings of Saturn, an experience that no one can ever forget. (If I'm not mistaken, it launched Isaac Asimov on a lifelong interest in astronomy, science, and science fiction.)

There was one thread of interest, though, that constantly grew and wound its way through most of my life, and that is a true love of electrical phenomena and electronics.

### High School/College

After graduating as the salutatorian of my junior high school, I was told that I should try out for Brooklyn Tech (a specialized science high school in my hometown of Brooklyn, New York). I did, and I did well there, ultimately leading to a scholarship to Columbia University, where I studied to be an electrical engineer, receiving BSEE and MSEE degrees. The scholarship also earned me an internship at the Bell Telephone Laboratories, or Bell Labs. There I started a career of invention, generating several patents while designing state-of-the-art telecommunications equipment and ultimately becoming an engineering supervisor. Interestingly enough, what really helped me along was the knowledge I had gained from all the gadgets and makeshift prototypes I built as a child and young man.

Later on (at the breakup of the Bell system in 1984) I moved from Bell Labs to Bell Communications

*Research, or "Bellcore," which did the research
for essentially all of the U.S. telecommunications
network. I had a great deal of fun there, and again
generated many new ideas and a lot of patents
(twenty-seven by the time I left Bell). I became an
executive director at Bellcore and invented a device
called the Electronic Panning Camera.*

*That device led to an interview with Disney, where
I have been happily working for the last fifteen years.
I have enjoyed my career here and am currently the
only Disney Research Fellow. I have been fortunate
enough to have contributed a number of technologies
to numerous attractions in the theme parks and have
increased my patent portfolio by another thirty or so
inventions. I have also had the good fortune to be
able to continue to do what I love to do. I know my
father would be proud if he were still around!*

\* \* \* \* \* \* \* \* \* \*

**Eddie Sotto** created projects for the Disney Parks and
Resorts for thirteen years before forming his own company—
SottoStudios. His "show biz" approach is especially note-
worthy—he was born in Hollywood and was inspired by his
aunt, film and theme park costume designer Marilyn Sotto-
Erdmann, and mentored by Herb Ryman and other Disney
Legends. Eddie is most proud of Pooh's Hunny Hunt at Tokyo
Disneyland because "it was the first 'trackless' dark ride with
vehicles that interact with one another." The technology paved
the way for Mystic Manor in Hong Kong Disneyland and other
"E-ticket attractions." Eddie says he's excited to see Disney
continuing to "go places no mouse has gone before!"

*My father once said, "Play is work that you like to do." I have found that the first use of creativity is to find something to enjoy in whatever you are doing. We seldom get "masterpieces" to work on, and in the meantime we hone our skills.*

*You apply your creative process to solving in new ways. Getting paid to learn, no matter what you are doing, helps you to be content and to push further. Spending six years of your life designing a Main Street (in Disneyland Paris) that had been done elsewhere was, at times, creatively depressing. To creatively thrive, you mine what could be reinvented, question the status quo. I had wanted to design rides, but in lieu of that rightfully convinced myself that Main Street was the ultimate dining and retail center, and by learning all aspects of retail and restaurant design I would master a very valuable skill to be used later. As life would have it, that experience was leveraged in designing successful restaurants and retail after leaving Disney. All made possible by mentally turning the potentially derivative work of "Main Street" into an opportunity to "play."*

\* \* \* \* \* \* \* \* \* \*

**Mickey Steinberg** was an established and recognized pro-fessional executive when he joined Imagineering in 1988 as executive vice president and chief operating officer. Born in Augusta, Georgia, and achieving bachelor of science and bachelor of architecture degrees from Georgia Tech, and a master of architecture from MIT, he had spent twenty-seven years managing one of the grand architecture, planning, and development firms, The Portman Companies of Atlanta, before becoming an Imagineer. His favorite experience during his six years at Disney: "Reorganizing Imagineering to place the right people in leadership positions at all levels, empowering them to be decision makers, and then working with them to create incredible projects on time and on budget."

*When I was eleven, I contracted polio and I spent nearly a year at the Warm Springs Center in Georgia undergoing rehabilitation treatment. We had a lot of free time, and I, along with a few other young patients, spent as much time as we could around the construction sites where new buildings were being constructed. We saw that the man in charge was the architect who visited the site once a week. He let us hang around, and he would describe to us what was happening.*

*He explained to us that he believed that if they created buildings that were light and cheerful in which we, the patients, lived and were treated, that our chances of recovery were much greater. He explained that he felt a cheerful environment was the most effective tool for ensuring recovery. To a young boy, this was hard for me to understand, but when I was moved into a new dorm that had been completed, I was much happier and more enthusiastic about the treatment, and I did recover. I decided then that I wanted to be an architect and create great places that would affect people's lives.*

*While attending high school, I took architectural drafting courses and I worked for an architect in my spare time. I started by keeping the office clean and maintaining the supplies, but by the time I graduated, I was working on construction documents for homes. The architects in the office discussed the spaces they were creating and how people would react to them, and it was interesting to see that some of our houses actually did affect people in ways that they had discussed.*

*I went to Georgia Tech and studied architecture, and after graduation I went in the Army for four years. When I left the service, I returned to school and received graduate degrees in architecture and structural engineering from Georgia Tech and MIT.*

*After a few years, I finally convinced John Portman, Fellow of the American Institute of Architects (FAIA), who was a young architect who I thought was creating really great buildings, to hire me. He was a maverick who decided that if he was going to create really wonderful buildings with innovative spaces, he would have to develop them himself, as owners did not want to gamble on building projects with new ideas. Portman constantly explained that he was creating buildings for the people who used them and not for architectural critics. Over time, our projects, although sometimes controversial, were recognized for their innovative spaces, and people responded positively to our projects.*

*I was with Portman for twenty-seven years, and during that time we designed and developed projects in various parts of the world. We felt that we were affecting people's lives with the projects we were* developing. I had become one of the key people in The Portman Companies by that time and I was now the man on the sites leading the effort to improve people's lives by what we were building.

I lived in Atlanta and visited Walt Disney World many times over the years. My children responded to Walt Disney World as if they had actually experienced the real worlds that the Imagineers had created. My sister-in-law could not visit Epcot enough, as she said that since she could not travel the world, she felt that she had actually experienced these wonderful places by spending time at the World Showcase. I believed that no one excelled at creating places that affected people's lives and their well-being through the use of our imagination and creativity as did the Imagineers.

In 1988, I accepted the opportunity to join the Imagineers in a leadership role. I then joined the ranks of the most in-depth, versatile group of people, who were creating projects that have a huge impact on the imagination and attitude of the people who experience them. I then learned from the Imagineers a new phrase that incorporated what that first architect was trying to capture. The term was "suspension of disbelief." It meant to him that these spaces he created helped us believe that we could get well, although the general belief of the time was no one overcame polio. However, if we could be influenced in suspending disbelief, if just for a little while, and believe that we would recover, our beliefs would have a big impact on us. No one can create spaces that allow you to suspend disbelief better *than the Imagineers. For a short time, children really believe they are in a magic land, even though they really know they are in Florida. For a short while, my sister-in-law believed that she was in Paris when she really knew she was in Florida. People in Portman buildings believed they were in some special place even though they knew they were in Atlanta or New York or wherever.*

*To work with people who can create such places that affect people's lives, even for a short time, is exciting and a wonderful experience. Imagineers suspend disbelief while they are actually working and believe that they are just having a wonderful time fantasizing with the most talented people anywhere about creating magical places for everyone to enjoy.*

* * * * * * * * * *

**Dorisz Tatar** was born in Budapest, Hungary. She studied scenic design at Kennesaw State University in Georgia and received her master of fine arts in scenic painting at CalArts. An associate dimensional designer with two years at Imagineering (one as an intern), her favorite project was "painting the overall scale model of the Shanghai Disneyland Park. I realized how many disciplines have to work together to bring such a massive story to life and create magic. It's what Imagineering is all about."

*My passion is telling stories, and color is one of the most powerful visual elements in narrative development. Color just makes me happy. It's that simple. Sharing my passion during a CalArts showcase* at Imagineering led me to an internship and eventually to become a full-time Imagineer.

The journey wasn't easy. While pursuing my masters degree in fine arts, some people were very skeptical. They all thought it was a bad idea, and that no decent job would ever come of it, not one that I can live off of, anyway. But they were all wrong. And you know what the funny thing is? I knew that all along. I never listened to them; their criticism never got me down, because I believed in my passion.

For all of you artistic dreamers out there, below are some helpful lessons that I learned along the way. I hope you shoot for the stars!

1. Don't ever take no for an answer.
2. Don't get discouraged. People get turned down many times before they get their big break. Being turned down just means that it wasn't your time. Get right back up—and believe in yourself.
3. When going on an interview, don't try to cater to what they want to hear. Talk about what you love doing and what makes you happy.
4. When you are truly passionate about something, it radiates. Others will notice and your work will speak for itself.

\* \* \* \* \* \* \* \* \* \*

**Bob Weis,** executive vice president and creative portfolio leader of the Shanghai Disney Resort project, has spent twenty-five years at Imagineering creating attractions and environments from Tokyo to Orlando (he led the development of Disney's Hollywood Studios). Born in Pomona, California,

Bob received his bachelor of science degree in architecture from Cal Poly Pomona. In answer to the "favorite project" question, he responded: "That's a tough one, as I've been lucky to work on so many fascinating jobs. I am now working on what will only be the sixth 'castle park' in Disney history. For an Imagineer to lead a 'Disneyland,' and to be able to reinvent it in a dynamic place like China—I guess that's tough to beat. The historic and cultural significance of it is pretty amazing."

*I worked for one summer at Disneyland in 1976. There I gained a sense of pride in being part of Disney and learned a lot by walking Disneyland and seeing how it all worked. I also heard about an elite, mysterious group called WED (which later became Walt Disney Imagineering).*

*I left that summer job and heard nothing more about WED until I was finishing my senior project—a joint theater and architecture thesis. WED had appeared at Cal Poly for recruiting and I met with a representative, almost by accident.*

*Once I drove out and saw WED, I decided that was the only place for me—a diverse group of artists and designers working in a bunch of warehouses crammed with models and mock-ups. I admit I was terribly lucky to get hired right out of school. But I was to first be a coordinator, not a designer of any kind, on a "lifted" project, the first foreign park, Tokyo Disneyland.*

*I set myself about trying to learn everything I could about the Imagineering process and to meet as many talented people as possible. And that is the advice I give every Imagineer. Imagineering is like a compact university. It's filled with interesting people and strange departments. The more you can learn about all of them, the more you have a chance to innovate and excel. Later, the knowledge I gained from wandering the halls helped me lead design on Disney's Hollywood Studios, the concept for Tokyo DisneySea, and the first Disney park in Shanghai.*

*My foreign experience taught me that Imagineering is also enriched by being open to the outside. Keeping your sights set on everything that is happening—inside and outside Disney—is critical. Walt was a great assimilator; he traveled, and he brought in diverse minds to think about ideas.*

*You don't have to be at Imagineering to do this; everywhere there are artists, labs, tinkerers, and interesting new projects to visit and experience. Record them in your notes or sketchbook, and think about how they might apply to future ideas.*

*I do believe everything great "takes a village" to do it, so build yours wide and diverse, inside and out. When it comes time to do the impossible, you'll be glad you've got all those crazy minds around you.*

*My favorite quote:*

*Q: How many Imagineers does it take to screw in a lightbulb?*
*A: Why does it have to be a lightbulb?*

\* \* \* \* \* \* \* \* \* \*

**Coulter Winn,** an architecture executive, was born in Norfolk, Virginia, and attended the University of California,

Berkeley. In his twenty-four years at Imagineering, he developed iconic design projects that include the Tower of Terror in Disneyland Paris, Penny's Bay train station in Hong Kong Disneyland, the American Waterfront in Tokyo DisneySea, and Sunset Boulevard in Disney's Hollywood Studios in Walt Disney World. Coulter's newest project is the centerpiece of the Shanghai Disneyland Park, the Enchanted Storybook Castle. His previous favorite: Buena Vista Street in Disney California Adventure, because "it successfully transformed the park's entrance into a fun, immersive environment that connected the story of the park with the story of Walt Disney's life."

*On November 5, 1990, I found myself in Imagineering's "Big D" cafeteria with twenty fellow "New Imagineers" to meet Marty Sklar and John Hench. Hench asked if there were any architects in the group. I raised my hand. John then asked me if I knew what Walt Disney's four levels of detail were. I said no, so he told me: "Detail level one is when you are standing out in the countryside and see the church steeple sticking up above the trees. Detail level two is when you enter town and are looking down the street. You can see the street, the median, the parkway strips, sidewalks, and trees. Detail level three is when you are standing on the sidewalk looking at one of the houses. You can see the character of the house, walls, roof, windows, trim, and doors. Detail level four is when you have actually walked up to the front door, grabbed the door knocker, see its detail finish, and feel its temperature* and weight as you knock on the door. . . . Most architects are pretty good at getting to detail level three, but here at Disney we must always get to detail level four so we can maintain our immersive environments that support the stories we create."

I have found that advice to be true on every project I have worked on.

Suggestions for potential Imagineering architects . . . sketch and doodle, note the things you like—the shape of a chimney or some form which is pleasing. Why do you like it? Conversely, what about things you don't like, that bother you? You don't have to be a real critic; just think about things. Field sketching or painting is a great way to do this since you really have to look at the subject at hand. That is when I really start to analyze it. Generally we sketch things we like. . . . What about things you don't? That ugly alleyway or utility pole— can you draw the subject in a way that makes it look better? What did you do to it in the process? Fun little games like that will help you develop your art sensibilities, which are important at WDI. Study proportion and composition theory as well. There are a variety of books out there.

A lot of students want to come to WDI straight out of school. I didn't, and I would recommend others don't either. What we do here is specialized. Experience in the broader practice can be very beneficial and make you more valuable when you do join Imagineering.

\* \* \* \* \* \* \* \* \* \*

**Doris Hardoon Woodward** was born and raised in Hong Kong—both parents are Shanghainese and moved to Hong Kong in 1949. After graduating with BFA honors in graphics from the California College of the Arts in Oakland, she came to Imagineering in 1979 to work on Epcot's The Land pavilion. Doris is now the senior director/executive producer for the Shanghai Disney Resort (proving that you can go home again!). Her favorite project: an unrealized West Coast version of Epcot for Anaheim called Westcot "for the story richness, diversity, texture, first-time concepts, the international content, the incredible team that believed in the concepts— we had the best time working together!" Doris's advice comes in six bullet points:

- *Pass on the Secret—IT ALL STARTS WITH A STORY!*
- *Stay with your passion.*
- *Stay confident with your hopes and dreams.*
- *Don't let others sway you from your responsibilities and vision.*
- *When still in school, get as much internship experience as possible.*
- *"The first step is the hardest, and if opportunity doesn't knock, build a door!"*

\* \* \* \* \* \* \* \* \* \*

**Susan Zavala**—another "local" Southern Californian born in Glendale—attended Glendale Community College, Pasadena City College, Valencia Community College, and Art Center College of Design in Pasadena. With twenty-five years' experience at many different tasks at Imagineering, Susan is now a design asset specialist—meaning she is part of a team that helps to find and then implement new digital systems and processes. Her newest assignment is her favorite: "The things we are doing with new technology will assist every Imagineer daily to work more efficiently and collaboratively."

*I first walked through the magical world of Disney and Imagineering in 1988 on a temporary assignment. I brought with me raw creative talent, a huge desire to learn, enormous enthusiasm, and a willingness to continue my schooling. After a very short time, I was hired and placed into a department that supported the artists and creative division behind the scenes with their live presentations throughout the company and the world.*

*I continued my education with a focus on art, business, and then computer technology; I changed majors a few times and attended colleges here in California and in Orlando, when I lived there as an Imagineer for over five years after my first initial six years in California.*

*I have been back in California since 2000, and over the years my career has taken a most wonderful, unexpected, organic, creative, challenging, exciting, and unique route. My title has changed many times over the years and I have worn the hats of assisting, creating, producing, innovating, entertaining, dreaming, encouraging, and appreciating, many times all in the same day.*

*Whether you have a solid dream you are pursuing currently or are wondering just what's out there in that big ol' world that appeals to you most, I can share this with you from my own experience: don't be surprised if the thing you are striving for takes a different shape than what you had first imagined. The rewards may be the same: teamwork, brainstorming, innovating, creating, fun . . . it's just that the environment you do it in may be new and unexpected to you.*

*Change is a constant and can be one of the most exhilarating experiences of your life. Walt Disney would have been the first to tell you to "Be Curious about Everything . . ." So, always ask questions. Try and look at the ordinary and familiar in new, cutting-edge and inventive ways. Seek out the best in people and be willing to join many teams. Never give up on yourself and go easy if you have impatience. Never stop learning and have a good attitude while you are. Keep your notebooks and sketch pads with you, and remember how creative and brilliant you are ('cuz you are!). Above all, don't forget to have fun, and if you find you are running into any roadblocks, please know there are multiple solutions to any problem; maybe the world is just waiting for you to invent something entirely new!*

*May your dreams all come true, your journey be showered with unexpected miracles, and your life be better than you could have ever imagined for yourself!*

\* \* \* \* \* \* \* \* \* \*

In starting this project months ago, it was my hope to make it much more than a letter from Marty about The Road to

Imagineering. On the previous pages, you have seen how well my hopes and dreams were realized with the participation of seventy-five Imagineers.

Knowing how busy they are with new and old projects in every part of the world—not just on land but also at sea, and not just theme parks and resort hotels but technical and research and development support for other parts of Disney—I was hesitant to ask the two "chiefs" of the Imagineers to play in this sandbox. But I finally did ask—very late in the game—and both responded: "We want to play, too!"

To conclude the We Get Letters . . . section, here are the thoughts and experiences of Imagineering's leadership:

\* \* \* \* \* \* \* \* \* \*

**Craig Russell** is a thirty-one-year Imagineer with a degree in engineering from UCLA. Born in Lancaster, California, he is responsible for the design of all construction drawings and then building from them—thus his title: chief design and project delivery executive. His favorite projects: both Tokyo parks (Tokyo Disneyland and Tokyo DisneySea). Craig is a leader in community service; he has volunteered and served as an officer of Habitat for Humanity in Southern California.

### Advice to an Aspiring Imagineer

*Advice I'm fond of giving to those who believe they want to be an Imagineer:*

- *There is not a particular curriculum or list of majors that uniquely prepares one for Imagineering. We are a broad* collection of diverse artistic, technical, and management talents—theater designers and technicians, architects, fine artists, engineers, scientists, builders, and managers who together create amazing experiences.

- All of our talents and everything we do are in service of story. We are a creatively driven studio in which the best idea will flourish.
- Imagineering is at its core a team sport requiring high-impact collaboration. Those in search of individual contribution or credit are most often frustrated in our studio. Imagineers who make those around them successful most often flourish.
- Imagineers are teachers with a deep understanding that we cannot realize our amazing projects alone. We also possess the drive to evolve our projects to remain relevant and evolve how we realize those projects so that we can maximize our global impact.
- Imagineers settle for nothing less than excellence. This is not a studio for people interested in an easy job; it's a place where passion and excellence result in extraordinary accomplishments.

Most of all, Imagineering is a place for those who want to dedicate their energy to create happiness for hundreds of millions of people around the world. At Imagineering, we have a simple statement of belief that happy people make the world a better place. We have the privilege and responsibility to create happiness on a global scale. A career here is far from the easiest job you can find, but it will without a doubt be one of the most challenging and rewarding things you can dedicate yourself to.

* * * * * * * * * *

**Bruce Vaughn** became Imagineering's chief creative executive (my job for thirty years!) in 2007. Born in a town "steeped in literary tradition"—Sag Harbor, New York—Bruce graduated with a degree in fine arts from Colgate University and started out to become a lawyer before "finding my true passion in the entertainment industry." His favorite project at Imagineering? "The one I'm working on, of course! If I have to pick one, it would be the Disney Cruise Line ships, the *Dream* and *Fantasy*. For me, no project embodies every aspect of what Imagineering does in a more integrated way. The staterooms, restaurants, pools, live shows, merchandise, kids clubs, and deck activities all relate to each other like no other park or experience we create. We even get to design the crew quarters and living areas, since our crew is the only cast that lives with us! These ships are one thousand feet long, weigh 140,000 tons, and accommodate over five thousand guests and crew. And they are beautiful, whimsical, and fun! Quintessential Disney."

"*Imagineering? That's not even a word!*"
*The Disney human resources representative looked puzzled at my response to her telling me the name of the organization that had acquired the small visual-effects company I was working for in 1993.*
"*You're an Imagineer now!*"
*Her enthusiasm told me I should be really excited and honored with my new job. I had no idea. Unlike so many Imagineers I would come to know and work*

with over the next twenty-plus years, I had not heard of Imagineering. In fact, when asked what my favorite Disney attraction was my first week on the job, I honestly answered that I had never been to a Disney park. I grew up in New York. Our family trips were to Civil War battlefields, museums, or to see family. I immediately found myself on a plane to Orlando with a long list of attractions and shows to see.

That first visit to Walt Disney World was truly eye-opening. Granted, it was a little strange to be alone in a place designed for group experiences, but the scale, attention to detail, and epic nature of the whole place humbled me. That evening I called my parents and said, "You were almost the perfect parents. Had you taken me to ride Peter Pan when I was nine years old, you would have earned superhero status for life!"

I returned from that trip a believer in the power of design and the nobility in creating places that make people happy. I also became a student of Imagineering. So much more than a company, Imagineering is a culture. This culture was born of the genius of a remarkable innovator and a handpicked collection of multi-disciplined entertainment wizards. They invented a unique design process rooted in optimism, a can-do spirit, and belief that there are no bad people, that everyone shares the desire to be happy, and that good design will bring out the best in people. We walk humbly in their footsteps, adhering to the process and beliefs they set forth over sixty years ago.

Though there are over 140 disciplines within

Imagineering, all Imagineers have one thing in common: they love what they do. Imagineers follow their hearts. They do not show up at the offices or construction sites around the world because it's a job; they do so because being an Imagineer is the best way to put their imaginations and creativity to use. Imagineers are passionate.

There is not one path to becoming an Imagineer or being an Imagineer. I studied English literature and fine arts in college. The Imagineer in the office next to me studied mechanical engineering, but now manages our creative directors and producers. For years, I sat next to our chief scientist, who has degrees in civil engineering, a PhD in environmental science, is fluent in French and Mandarin, and plays blues guitar. My experiences as an Imagineer have included working on things as diverse as writing a short film for a pavilion at Epcot, an Audio-Animatronics walking dinosaur named Lucky, leading our Research and Development group, and my current role as chief creative executive. I never could have anticipated doing any of these things. It turns out studying Shakespeare was the perfect path for me to become the Imagineer I am.

Imagineers are multi-dimensional individuals who bring many assets to the table. What they studied in school is only a part of the value they bring. Just as important is their diversity of thought, and their hobbies and experiences outside of the office. Imagineers love the richness of the world. Imagineers are explorers who are fascinated by the variety of cultures, vastness of nature, and diversity of this wonderful universe.

Imagineers are both experts in certain disciplines, as well as endlessly curious about subjects they know little about. Curiosity, passion, and a sense of adventure and wonder are all typical attributes of Imagineers. We never stop being students, and never tire of learning something new.

When asked what to study to become an Imagineer, my answer is simple: study what you are most passionate about. Travel the world every opportunity you can. Stop and reflect on the places you visit every day. Even the most mundane experiences are opportunities to learn. Think about designing for happiness everywhere you go, and dream of ways that everyday experiences can be more satisfying.

Many people believe Imagineers are theme park ride designers. We design attractions, this is true. We also design live theater shows, spectaculars, hotels, cruise ships, marketplaces, restaurants, bathrooms, vehicles, light fixtures . . . you name it, an Imagineer can and probably has designed it. But all of that is in service of our true product: the guest experience.

That's right, Imagineers design the places for people to have happy experiences and create cherished memories that last a lifetime. How do you study for that? Just follow your heart, be curious, dream, and be obsessed with making things real.

Oh, and never lose the connection to that child inside of you. That child is your best guide to making *your dreams come true. Follow your heart and somehow, some way, you will realize the happy life you seek. If being an Imagineer remains your dream, I'm sure I'll see you on one of our teams helping make the world a better place by making people happy.*

NCE OF TREATMENT, PROVIDE A TON OF TREAT
STOP LEARNING • I TELL ONE STORY
SUAL MAGNET) • COLLABOR
TY • I KNOW YOUR A
TAIN IDENTIT
IENC

# THE LAST WORD

When I asked the Imagineers if they would "write a paragraph, several paragraphs, or a full page—no more—about what you now know that will help young people who think they want careers in your field," little did I know that, for some, I was opening floodgates to pent-up memories and advice. For quite a few, that meant more than one page. And for at least one, what came back to me was the treatment for his dissertation for a doctoral degree in theme park design!

Well, not really—but I did accuse Kevin Rafferty of exactly that when I received his seven-page note!

Born in Hollywood, Kevin graduated from California State University, Fullerton, with the idea that he would become an animator. But as you read earlier under the banner of "Disney Park Experience," his Disney career began inauspiciously as a dishwasher in the Plaza Inn at Disneyland! That was thirty-six years ago.

Today—several years after his leading role in creating

Cars Land, and especially Radiator Springs Racers at Disney California Adventure—Kevin is an executive creative director leading the design and development of a proposed new second gate park in Hong Kong—so secret (code-named "Project Happy") it had still not been announced as this book was being written and going to press.

Kevin's talent as a writer, producer, and developer of new concepts is the stuff of . . . well, legendary Disney projects. I think of Kevin Rafferty as the prototypical Imagineer—selfless team player, a wellspring of creative ideas, teacher of young talent. He represents so many of the traits I have written about in this book: he is passionate, loves to collaborate, is sought after as a mentor, and is always stretching to dream up new concepts . . . and do them!

When I read Kevin's seven-page "essay," I realized it was the perfect way to end this book. And so, for "The Last Word," I am privileged to present "What I Know Now I Wish I Knew Then," by Imagineer **Kevin Rafferty**:

**What I Know Now I Wish I Knew Then**

Marty Sklar often said Walt Disney had one foot in the past and one in the future. That's exactly where I feel like I'm standing right now as a longtime Imagineer. When I began my career at WED Enterprises in 1978, there were only two Disney theme parks in the world. Now there are eleven, not to mention water parks, resorts, cruise ships, and much more. Along the way, Imagineering has had plenty of hits and a few misses. After all these years, I've come to the conclusion that carefully evaluating and learning from our past successes and failures before designing for the future is essential. Knowing what worked, what didn't, and why should inform our every step forward.

There's a huge difference between *learning from the past* and *living in the past*. Some folks want Imagineers to re-create things that are no longer in existence exactly the way they fondly remember them: among them, Tomorrowland, 1967. But ironically, rebuilding Tomorrowland exactly the way it was almost fifty years ago would make it "Yesterdayland," and bringing back this land of tomorrow today would be living in the past. For today's Imagineers, keeping yesterday's lessons in our designs for tomorrow would serve us well.

What was at the heart of the projects from the past people loved so much they want brought back? And what is at the core of our most recent projects that make them so successful? The answer to both of these questions can be found in the fundamental design principles established by our Imagineering predecessors. This is not to say we should approach everything from an old-fashioned perspective and dream and do nothing new.

But these timeless principles still apply today. Storytelling is as old as humankind because humans always have new stories to tell. The best and most memorable stories always have a fundamental, common structure at their core. It took many years to solidify my thoughts about the perfect formula for creating a successful new attraction or whole park, and it all boils down to thoughtful, well-executed theater brought to life upon the foundation of our tried-and-true design principles (and a few new ones). In a word: showmanship.

## Sincerity and Truth

It's okay to make believe, but it's not okay to *fake* believe. When Disney California Adventure opened, our guests were greeted at the entrance by a stylized Golden Gate Bridge, a sharp and pointed metallic sun sculpture floating above an "ocean" wave confined in a box, and contemporary popular music, much like the kind you may have listened to in your car moments before arriving at the park. The Disney California Adventure park on opening day was the result of a grand experiment in fresh and different "build it and they will come" thinking.

Our guests did indeed come, but many were disappointed because they were expecting to go to another place in another time, just as they had always done at Disneyland. Nothing about the California Adventure Park's entrance suggested they were anywhere really. The later, much-needed addition of Buena Vista Street to the park changed all that because it brought to the entrance a warm and welcoming *real* place in another time. Although we entirely invented Buena Vista Street, it is sincere in its placemaking and believable because every design cue and detail was informed and inspired by a real place from a real time: the time when Walt arrived in Los Angeles with a cardboard suitcase in his hand and a dream in his heart.

There are no sharp and pointy metallic edges, no contradictions, visual intrusions, or stylized anything that take you out of this story. It is pure showmanship that, like Disneyland, sets up the park story and embraces you with the warm and welcome reassurance that it's okay to leave your worldly cares behind and enter into the magic.

**Time and Money**

Never let budget drive the idea. Let the idea drive the idea. That doesn't mean you should be a loose cannon and not consider the cost. You must be responsible and work to an established budget. But good design is good design no matter what the dollar figure. Our guests will never say, "I love that attraction because the Imagineers delivered it on time and on budget." Our guests will love the attraction because it's great and it makes them feel great.

If for any reason during the evolution of a project you feel like you're heading toward delivering mediocrity, budget-wise or otherwise, bail out. Regroup. Rethink. Always plan to deliver nothing less than excellence.

**Hub and Spoke**

Our Magic Kingdom castle parks work well from a circulation and way-finding standpoint because they follow the original Disneyland lead of the "Hub and Spoke" design. The castle, as a compelling icon, draws us down Main Street to a hub that is centrally located in the park. Radiating out from the hub, like spokes on a wheel, are pathways leading out to the outlying lands. Now that everyone knows "all roads" lead back to the castle, it becomes the North Star, which helps you to navigate your way back home. That's why you tell your family and friends, "Meet you at the castle at noon."

For many years our guests had long been used to the ease of way-finding and destination decision-making. We had made the course clear for them. But when Disney's Animal Kingdom opened, the entrance sequence caused great confusion. The pathways meandered and the surrounding landscape was visually obstructive, so the way was not clear. The design intent was to quickly immerse you into the dense foliage of a natural world, but the intended promise of discovery and adventure was ironically superseded by way-finding woes. Providing no clear pathway or iconic visual "wienie" to draw you forward is, to me, going backward.

**Stick to the Rules**

*Always* be true to the time and place you are creating, in every way, shape, and form. No matter how simple a rule-breaking visual contradiction, it can throw everything off. One day I was in Frontierland at Disneyland and the "long shot" to the general store maintained its believability, which kept me in that time and place. But as I stepped closer, over the horseshoe prints in the ground, onto the perfectly detailed old west boardwalk, I was suddenly lassoed back into today. Why? Featured in the window of this period-correct old west general store was a spinner rack upon which were displayed dozens of pink rubber flip-flops. What in tarnation? Somebody call the sheriff!

## Teamwork

Ronald Reagan said, "It is amazing what you can accomplish if you do not care who gets the credit." Forget about credit. Leave any desire for notoriety at the door with your ego. Our best attractions have been those that have been delivered by a close-knit team that shared a vision and relied upon each other to deliver the best possible guest experience. When a team inspires and encourages each other and is motivated only by the strength and promise of a great idea, magic happens. One spark plug will not get a car moving. Teamwork is the engine that will get you there.

## Listen

*Listen* to the needs and wants of the parks. It's okay to design blue-sky stuff just because it's fun to do, but oftentimes the concepts will go into a drawer unless there's a desire by the park for something like it. Blizzard Beach was built because Walt Disney World needed another water park. Toy Story Midway Mania! was built because the Disneyland Resort wanted another family game attraction.

*Listen* to your colleagues. Respect their thoughts and notes and react to them accordingly. We are all in it together, even if we aren't working on the same projects. When Imagineering fails, we all fail. When Imagineering is successful, we are all successful.

*Listen* to your leaders. Even if at first you don't agree or see the value of receiving their notes and direction, be open-minded. During the early development of Animal Kingdom Park, I pitched an idea to Michael Eisner for a show in which Rafiki, the sage from *The Lion King*, presented an insightful overview of the animal kingdom inside the Tree of Life. Michael didn't buy it. Instead he suggested doing a show about insects. To that I thought to myself, "Now why would we do a show about bugs in a park about animals?"

Remaining open-minded, I was shocked when I opened the first page of the first book I selected to begin researching bugs. It read "The 10 quintillion insects in the world make up 80% of the Animal Kingdom."

*Listen* to yourself. If your gut tells you there's something mediocre or not quite right about a project you are pitching or working on, or if your gut tells you it will be something fun and special, it's correct in both cases. Never work on or pitch an idea you're not crazy about. And if you create and/or pitch several options to your idea, make sure you'd be willing to deliver your least favorite one. Better yet, don't even have a least favorite one.

## Research, Research, and More Research!

Become an expert on the topic, characters, place, time, and theme of every project you are working on. Research informs, inspires, and fuels an idea and helps to make it authentic.

**The One-Liner**

From an ideation perspective, the hardest thing to do is to distill down into one sentence the description and story for an idea. When you can do this, it means you've done the hard part, the difficult groundwork required to totally understand what it's all about. Having done your homework, you can now clearly communicate the idea to others.

Michael Eisner, once a creative executive at ABC, was the one to whom writers gave their "elevator pitches" for made-for-TV movies. Fascinated by this distillation process, I once asked him if he could recall the fastest, easy-to-get pitch that got him to instantly green-light a movie idea. "Okay," he responded. "Here's the idea: 'An airplane filled with blind passengers crashes on a mountaintop and they have to find their way down.'"

Got it. Blizzard Beach Water Park: "A ski resort is built after a freak snowstorm in central Florida, but once the tropical sun returned, it caused the ski runs to melt."

**Quick-Read Visual Storytelling**

Brevity is key to good theme park design. Sometimes you only have four minutes to tell an attraction's entire story. At Mystic Manor in Hong Kong Disneyland, there's a perfect little visual storytelling moment that helps set up the story for the attraction. Across from the manor, within clear view of the queue, is a small railroad station from which a track spur leads directly over to the "deliveries" platform behind the manor. On the spur track is a cargo handcart upon which are exotic antiquities being delivered to the manor. The attraction story is about a collection of antiquities that come to life.

You simply cannot write a two-hundred-page backstory and expect anyone to understand how all of that factors into an idea. Learn to toss out the stuff you love to make the story better, clearer, easy to get. Use less character dialogue in favor of more action and quick-read visual storytelling. Each scene in Radiator Springs Racers is exactly 10.4 seconds. Mater drives out to greet each incoming car every 10.4 seconds, and does it again and again, all day, every day.

## Look for Storytelling Opportunities in Every Nook and Cranny

Imagineer Jason Grandt was tasked with making an interior doorway wider in a Pirates-themed shop at the Magic Kingdom in Walt Disney World. The request to widen the arched doorway was motivated by new safety requirements. Jason could have simply made the opening two feet wider and no one would have known the difference. But Jason used it as a great opportunity for storytelling. Today the door is wider. But the reason is because a cannonball, still lodged in the wall, created so much of an impact that it caused a two-foot-wide section of the wall to fall!

**Perfect Orchestration of All Show Elements**

The true art of Imagineering is achieved only when there is a perfect orchestration of all included project elements. There is richness in subtlety. Just because an Audio-Animatronics character is designed with a lot of functions, that doesn't mean it should be programmed to move like crazy to showcase all those movements. These are "actors" and actors perform—not just move.

Show-lighting instruments should only light and call attention to what you want the audience to see. If everything in a scene is lit equally, no one knows where to look. Stage a scene to allow the audience to focus on the most important moment. If they are in a ride vehicle, enter a scene, and have to look back over their shoulder to find the action or story beat, you have failed. Audio is a delicate balance. Background music, sound effects, and character dialogue must never compete with one another. Never showcase or call attention to technology for technology's sake. Technology should serve the attraction, not be the attraction.

**Good Theater**

The pure art of storytelling is to keep your audience under the "spell" at all times. If something doesn't look right or does anything to interrupt the immersive moment, you've failed. You don't have to spend a lot of money when clever theater design and staging will do the trick. If scenic paint will create the illusion of wooden wall panels or an entire cityscape seen through a window, you don't have to build it in dimension. If you have to build something in dimension, you have to build enough of it to make it believable.

Never draw attention to the areas where you don't want your audience to look. Large attractions come with ugly necessities like air-conditioning ducting, ceiling panels, and overhead conduit runs. If you want those ugly bits to go away, keep the eye-catching stuff away!

Great attractions come with a variation of cadence and rhythm, fast and slow parts, big spaces and small spaces. If a symphony were written with the same emotion and tone from beginning to end, the piece would be boring. Consistent art direction is key. Choose one visual-design vernacular and stick with it. If your attraction features four different styles of characters, for example, the believability of the experience is disrupted.

**Reassurance**

A great theme park attraction allows guests to experience something they would not usually experience in their every day lives. I would never go hang gliding, but I love Soarin' Over California because I can eliminate all fear and still get a sense of what hang gliding *feels* like.

**it's a small world**

Be respectful and create and design every experience for the enjoyment of all cultures and languages.

### Get Experience in the Field

Nothing informs good thinking, good problem-solving, and good design like experience in the field. To be the best you can possibly be, you must have experience on a team that takes a project all the way through to opening day. No amount of talent or intuition can come close to the experience gained on a project site.

### Know When to Stop Designing

Imagineering is a big machine that, once it gets started on producing a project, moves full speed ahead with focus, passion, and purpose. It takes many united brains and hands to bring a dream to life, so team members from every discipline must do their part to bring their perspective and expertise to all phases of a project.

Once that orchestra starts coming together, constant changes from creative can be costly and disruptive to all involved. It's okay to do a little "arm waving" as the project evolves because unexpected things always happen, but major changes and redirection brought on midstream means the idea was not rock-solid to begin with. Be smart about the up-front. Be thorough. Don't keep designing and overthinking after the design phase is over. Rally the troops around a good, solid idea and say, "We're going this way!"

### Responsible Design

It's one thing to come up with a great idea for an attraction, land, or whole park, but it's another to get it built. You have to do the math, the engineering, and the integration of all elements that have to share a space; and these are only the tip of the iceberg. For example, a Disney park on a busy day can host a population of fifty thousand guests. Although you may have the greatest idea for an attraction ever, if it can only accommodate twenty guests an hour it's not going to cut it. A comfortable guest is a happy guest. Think about shade, comfortable vehicles, ease of way-finding into and around a park, refreshment, and more. Good design is about problem-solving. Never say, "We'll do that later" or "We'll fix it in the field." Solve all of the problems way up front.

## Get It Right the First Time

Imagineering is hard. Our three-dimensional, totally immersive brand of entertainment is the most difficult of all forms of entertainment because we build it to last with brick and mortar. Unlike live theater where something can be changed overnight if it's not working, or a film that, if it bombs, can be pulled from the movie theaters, or a TV show that can be canceled after an unsuccessful season and forgotten about, our parks and attractions are a physical commitment. We have to get it right the first time, every time. But here's the wonderful part about that: since we don't design for a two-dimensional screen (where anything happens because it can), the more magical and astonishing we can make an experience in the physical world, the more magical it is!

JJJION — J URGANIZE THE FLU... JI FLUPLE AND...
ICE OF TREATMENT, PROVIDE A TON OF TREAT...
STOP LEARNING...I TELL ONE STORY...
ISUAL MAGNET) · COLLABOR...
TY · I KNOW YOUR A...
TAIN IDENTI...
IEN...

# AFTERWORD

You didn't really think I would let Kevin have "the last word," did you? We've been friends a long, long time—I'm partial to good dishwashers! But I really loved the way we closed my memoir, *Dream It! Do It! My Half-Century Creating Disney's Magic Kingdoms*. So I asked Wendy Lefkon, the editorial director for Disney Editions, if we could end *this* book the same way—with a challenge to each of you who love to "Take a Chance"—who can't wait for that next blank page:

**There Are Two Ways to Look at a Blank Sheet of Paper**

It became something of a cliché of my years at Imagineering. "There are two ways to look at a blank sheet of paper," I said. "You can see it as the most frightening thing in the world—because *you have to make the first mark* on it. Or you can see a blank page as the greatest opportunity—*you get to make the first mark* on it. You can let your imagination fly in any direction. You can create whole new worlds."

I didn't care that it became a cliché. I remembered that comment George Lucas made in a meeting about the Star Tours attraction: "Don't avoid the clichés," George said. "They are clichés because they work!"

We finally commemorated the importance of this approach in a nine-inch-by-twelve-inch sketchbook printed with the text and image on the following page. My friend, artist John Horny, provided the official story sketch. Beyond the initial copy, all the pages were blank.

## The Most Frightening Thing in the World

Go ahead—and do something exciting on the next page. I've left it blank for you. Here's your chance to be an Imagineer!

# ROSTER OF PARTICIPATING IMAGINEERS

This book would not have been possible without the written input I received from the following seventy-five present, retired, and former Imagineers. A big thank you to all!

Jess Allen
Alfredo Ayala
Glenn Barker
Chris Beatty
Yves Benyeta
Barry Braverman
Fintan Burke
Jim Clark
Oscar Cobos Jr.
Lori Coltrin
Paul Comstock
Dave Crawford
Brian Crosby
Tim Delaney
Debbie DelMar
John Dennis
Andy DiGenova
Stan Dodd
David Durham
Maggie Elliott
Eli Erlandson
Peggie Fariss
Dave Fisher
Tom Fitzgerald
Omar Fuentes

Laurence Gertz
Josh Gorin
Bob Gurr
George Head
Joe Herrington
Zsolt Hormay
Shelby Jiggetts-Tivony
Daniel Joseph
Daniel Jue
Michael Jung
Marty Kindel
Zofia Kostyrko-Edwards
Aileen Kutaka
Gordon Lemke
Kathy Mangum
Nelson Meacham
Steve Miller
Chris Montan
Tom Morris
Kym Murphy
Brian Nefsky
Larry Nikolai
John Olsen
Diego Parras
Abe Quibin

Kevin Rafferty
Tom Rodowsky
Joe Rohde
Chris Runco
Craig Russell
Diane Scoglio
George Scribner
Cory Sewelson
Steve "Mouse" Silverstein
Theron Skees
Lanny Smoot
Eddie Sotto
Mickey Steinberg
Dex Tanksley
Dorisz Tatar
Jim Thomas
Val Usle
Michael Valentino
Bruce Vaughn
John Verity
Bob Weis
Coulter Winn
Doris Hardoon Woodward
Owen Yoshino
Susan Zavala

# INDEX

NEVER STOP LEARNING • 7 TELL ONE STORY AT A TIME • BE CURIOUS • 8 AVOID CONTRADICTIONS—MAIN
NIE (VISUAL MAGNET) • COLLABORATION • 5 COMMUNICATE WITH VISUAL LITERACY • DISNEY PARK EXP
NTAIN IT)! • 1 KNOW YOUR AUDIENCE • STORY • 2 WEAR YOUR GUESTS' SHOES • PASSION • 3 ORGANIZE
—MAINTAIN IDENTITY • TAKE A CHANCE / THINK DIFFERENTLY • 9 FOR EVERY OUNCE OF TREATMENT, PROV
K EXPERIENCE • 6 AVOID OVERLOAD—CREATE TURN-ONS • EDUCATION—NEVER STOP LEARNING • 7 TELL O
NIZE THE FLOW OF PEOPLE AND IDEAS • MENTOR • 4 CREATE A WIENIE (VISUAL MAGNET) • COLLABORATIO
ROVIDE A TON OF TREAT • BECOME THE BEST • 10 KEEP IT UP (MAINTAIN IT)! • 1 KNOW YOUR AUDIENCE
LL ONE STORY AT A TIME • BE CURIOUS • 8 AVOID CONTRADICTIONS—MAINTAIN IDENTITY • TAKE A CHANC
BORATION • 5 COMMUNICATE WITH VISUAL LITERACY • DISNEY PARK EXPERIENCE • 6 AVOID OVERLOAD—
UDIENCE • STORY • 2 WEAR YOUR GUESTS' SHOES • PASSION • 3 ORGANIZE THE FLOW OF PEOPLE AND
AKE A CHANCE / THINK DIFFERENTLY • 9 FOR EVERY OUNCE OF TREATMENT, PROVIDE A TON OF TREAT • B
D OVERLOAD—CREATE TURN-ONS • EDUCATION—NEVER STOP LEARNING • 7 TELL ONE STORY AT A TIME • B
PEOPLE AND IDEAS • MENTOR • 4 CREATE A WIENIE (VISUAL MAGNET) • COLLABORATION • 5 COMMUN
OF TREAT • BECOME THE BEST • 10 KEEP IT UP (MAINTAIN IT)! • 1 KNOW YOUR AUDIENCE • STORY • 2 W
RY AT A TIME • BE CURIOUS • 8 AVOID CONTRADICTIONS—MAINTAIN IDENTITY • TAKE A CHANCE / THINK
• 5 COMMUNICATE WITH VISUAL LITERACY • DISNEY PARK EXPERIENCE • 6 AVOID OVERLOAD—CREATE TU
ORY • 2 WEAR YOUR GUESTS' SHOES • PASSION • 3 ORGANIZE THE FLOW OF PEOPLE AND IDEAS • MENTOR
THINK DIFFERENTLY • 9 FOR EVERY OUNCE OF TREATMENT, PROVIDE A TON OF TREAT • BECOME THE BEST
E TURN-ONS • EDUCATION—NEVER STOP LEARNING • 7 TELL ONE STORY AT A TIME • BE CURIOUS • 8 AVOI
MENTOR • 4 CREATE A WIENIE (VISUAL MAGNET) • COLLABORATION • 5 COMMUNICATE WITH VISUAL LITE
BEST • 10 KEEP IT UP (MAINTAIN IT)! • 1 KNOW YOUR AUDIENCE • STORY • 2 WEAR YOUR GUESTS' SHOE
• 8 AVOID CONTRADICTIONS—MAINTAIN IDENTITY • TAKE A CHANCE / THINK DIFFERENTLY • 9 FOR EVERY
UAL LITERACY • DISNEY PARK EXPERIENCE • 6 AVOID OVERLOAD—CREATE TURN-ONS • EDUCATION—NEVER
SHOES • PASSION • 3 ORGANIZE THE FLOW OF PEOPLE AND IDEAS • MENTOR • 4 CREATE A WIENIE (VISU
VERY OUNCE OF TREATMENT, PROVIDE A TON OF TREAT • BECOME THE BEST • 10 KEEP IT UP (MAINTAIN
—NEVER STOP LEARNING • 7 TELL ONE STORY AT A TIME • BE CURIOUS • 9 AVOID CONTRADICTIONS—MAI
ENIE (VISUAL MAGNET) • COLLABORATION • 5 COMMUNICATE WITH VISUAL LITERACY • DISNEY PARK EXP
NTAIN IT)! • 1 KNOW YOUR AUDIENCE • STORY • 2 WEAR YOUR GUESTS' SHOES • PASSION • 3 ORGANIZE
—MAINTAIN IDENTITY • TAKE A CHANCE / THINK DIFFERENTLY • 9 FOR EVERY OUNCE OF TREATMENT, PROV
K EXPERIENCE • 6 AVOID OVERLOAD—CREATE TURN-ONS • EDUCATION—NEVER STOP LEARNING • 7 TELL O
NIZE THE FLOW OF PEOPLE AND IDEAS • MENTOR • 4 CREATE A WIENIE (VISUAL MAGNET) • COLLABORATIO
ROVIDE A TON OF TREAT • BECOME THE BEST • 10 KEEP IT UP (MAINTAIN IT)! • 1 KNOW YOUR AUDIENCE
LL ONE STORY AT A TIME • BE CURIOUS • 8 AVOID CONTRADICTIONS—MAINTAIN IDENTITY • TAKE A CHANC
BORATION • 5 COMMUNICATE WITH VISUAL LITERACY • DISNEY PARK EXPERIENCE • 6 AVOID OVERLOAD—
UDIENCE • STORY • 2 WEAR YOUR GUESTS' SHOES • PASSION • 3 ORGANIZE THE FLOW OF PEOPLE AND